'Stu brings into any organization a powerful tool that provides a common language for everyone that touches a customer. *The Four People You Should Know* becomes the standard terminology your team will utilize not only in selling to prospective clients, but selling internally as well. Personally, as an 'Orange', I can't recommend him more!'

Ivan G. Boyd, Senior VP and CRO
GTESS Corporation, Dallas, Texas

'Stu's practical approach to improving communications isn't just for sales people. We've applied it with great success to improve the interaction of a large project team too. The all too typical situation of different people having different definitions of success was making communication, and progress, rather frustrating for everyone. Stu showed us how to identify the real needs and priorities of each member of the team and then how to communicate with each of them everyday focusing on exactly what was important to them. The difference is amazing – everyone is now pulling in the same direction, and most importantly each person thinks 'color' first, to keep communications running smoothly everyday. Stu's methodology is now part of the way we do business!'

Barbara Lancaster, President - LTC International, Inc.

Stu is one gifted teacher who can bring across his ideas very succinctly and clearly to his audience. His stint in Singapore was certainly a very memorable time for our industry. All the participants gave him a "thumbs up" for his sessions. They benefited greatly from his training and found the ideas about the four kinds of people "revealing."
I would certainly recommend Stu to any companies who want to boost the performance of their sales people. Please book him now!

Samuel Goh-Former President
Financial Services Management Association-Singapore

Using Stu's book to analyze the different personalities in our office (based on the four colors) has helped our administrative staff deal with personality issues and resolve employee conflicts. Sales reps have a new 'tool' in their belt in deciding on how to sell to different personality types. The seminar was enjoyed by all company employees and brought a bonding element that we had never achieved before. So many jobs – so many skills needed for each specialty- the personality test will be used as an aide in future hiring. It is my recommendation that you pick your day and invite Stu Schlackman to train your employees – and you – as soon as possible!

Sharon Harrison, President-Nations Residential Services
Dallas, Texas

I saw Stu Schlackman speak at MDRT in Anaheim where he presented to approximately 1000 members and received an outstanding response from everyone in the room. Stu's presentation style is both entertaining and very informative. Stu received a lot of questions following his presentation which is always a good sign that the audience were engaged and wanting more.

Ross Hultgren-Financial Planner
MDRT Australia, Chairman

Competitive Excellence provides a highly effective approach to identify, analyze and connect personality styles... thus optimizing the sales opportunity! It also represents an invaluable sale management tool to better understand your sale force thus enabling them to more effectively compete... and win. All of our producers have been through Stu's training and in 2006 our revenues increased 24.2% and new business was up 35%! Thank you!

Stephen B. Smith, President, Wm. Rigg Co.

If you are looking to motivate your sales team and add a new dimension to their sales skills, Stu's workshop is a must. He had our team enthused, excited and eager to go out and apply his concepts.

Howard Elias
Chairman/CEO- Wealth Advisory Group LLC

FOUR PEOPLE
YOU SHOULD KNOW

ALSO BY THE AUTHOR

Don't Just Stand There, Sell Something

The 180 Rule for The Art of Connecting

FOUR PEOPLE YOU SHOULD KNOW

STU SCHLACKMAN
FOREWORD BY
SCOTT SCHLACKMAN

BETTERWAY PUBLISHING

You can find information on Stu & Scott Schlackman's workshops, sign up for our newsletter, and order additional books (volume discounts available) at:

Stu and Scott's website: www.connecting4people.com

Stu's website: stu@stuschlackman.com

Scott's website: scott@scottschlackman.com

Published in the United States by:
    BetterWay Publishing
    P.O. Box 118046
    Carrollton, TX 75011
    info@betterwaypublishing.com
    www.betterwaypublishing.com

Printed in the United States of America

TABLE OF CONTENTS

PREFACE

We tend to view situations in sales and in life through our own eyes. Many times we experience winning a sale where everything just falls into place. We hit it off with the decision makers, they understand the value we provide, and they quickly appreciate that the return on the investment is good. The sale closes and we move on to the next opportunity. Everything happened the way we wanted it to – from *our* perspective and agenda. It was very convenient that the customer agreed with our view on the benefits of the products and services. But that doesn't happen every time.

A similar situation for the next opportunity, same value, same return on investment, yet a different set of decision makers participates and the sale doesn't close. We lose to the competition and we are surprised. Why should one sale close and not the other?

In my career, as a sales professional, team leader, and trainer, I have thought about this question a lot. I have come to understand that a large part of the answer lies in personality – the personality of the sales person, the personality of the customer, and the way those personalities interact.

Using this book will help you address this personality dimension that is often overlooked when we convey our message to customers, team members and leaders – understanding how personality styles impact people's view of situations and events and how they interact with others. There are many excellent personality tools that have been created over the years. The one thing I've noticed that is consistent with all the tools is that they focus on 'you'. How *you* behave and relate to other people, what *you* value, how *you* make decisions.

In this book, I will take your sales technique one step further towards consistent success. While it is important to understand your personality type as a baseline to better understanding your view of situations, it is just as important, to understand how you interact with the *other* personality types. This means discovering *their* personality and adjusting your behavior to reflect this new knowledge.

A special thanks to my good friends who supported the creation of this book. I owe a particular debt to Wedge Greene for his rewrite of this book and also for his help with my newsletters. Trevor Hayes who edited my first book in 2004, helped with suggestions for this one. Trevor and Wedge help me tune my voice; without them this would not be the book you have before you. But all tasks must come to an end and any remaining errors are my responsibility.

And of course this book would not have been possible without the total support of my loving wife Betty and her commitment to our family and our business; she is the true pillar of my life.

Writing a book is a challenge. Yet with the support of friends like mine it becomes a joy. I consider myself blessed with family, friends and colleagues who have helped deliver this book.

Stu Schlackman

FOREWORD

I've known Stu Schlackman for 57 years. That may sound like a long time, but it's actually not, as he's my older brother. What makes our relationship unique is the fact that just over the past few years we have begun to connect in a way that we never did in our younger years. In fact, up until now the only thing that we had in common was our shoe size. He always did things so fast and I was more cautious. Stu would take risks and I was careful. I like harmony and he loved when things were chaotic. So as youngsters and throughout our adult lives we both went our separate ways. However, over the past few years our relationship has grown both personally and professionally in a way that we would have never imagined.

One would think that our newfound closeness would come about through long discussions and working through our differences. Not at all! After all these years, a light bulb went off and that light bulb was a personality styles tool that my brother developed which is the major focus in his book. Thanks to this tool, I now have a much better understanding of my personality style and that of my brother's and everyone around me. Understanding each other's personality style has enabled us to value each other's differences versus having our differences alienate us. Our differences in personality have now bonded us in a way that we would never have imagined. We are a team!

Over the past 25 years our paths have gone very different ways. I have been traveling the world as a global executive building teams in 15 different countries. I've had the opportunity to work in different cultures and languages under diverse situations. I have always used my intuitive skills, my gut, to better understand people and help them connect to achieve goals. While I was successful, I must say that at times it was challenging and at the same time exhausting. Meeting new people in different cultures and trying to understand how and why they tick is not always easy. I always thought there must be some kind of assessment or tool that could help people connect. I've tried every tool imaginable available on the marketplace. While many of them are good, I always had a hard time applying them in real world situations. They were always too complex and cumbersome. In today's world, we need speed and tools that are easy to use. I always ended up going back to my gut reaction on how to connect with others. However, I was always on the lookout for reassurance on my intuition.

While I was out traveling the world, my brother unbeknownst to me, was developing a tool that did everything I was looking for. A tool that could quickly help people better understand their personality style and how their style can impact others. In addition, it enables people to identify the personality style of others. My brother's tool achieves this goal in ways I never thought imaginable. It does all of this and at the same time it is easy to use.

What makes this tool so special is that it is simple, easy to understand, and fast to implement. In today's environment, we do not have a second to lose. Stu's personality assessment provides results in 10 minutes. Remember, Stu likes to do things fast! While I am a skeptic and prefer to do everything intuitively, I was shocked at how accurate it was while being so quick. It has provided me with an invaluable resource to better understand the teams I'm working with and the individuals that I coach. The combination of my brother's tool and my intuition has enabled me to dramatically improve my leadership skills, build teams and connect so much better with those around me.

What's even more rewarding is that after 57 years, my brother and I have teamed up to produce seminars, coaching and consulting to help teams develop exceptional performance. It's called Connecting4people.com. We combine my global experience with his fabulous assessment tool to help individuals and teams connect like never before.

Stu has been working in sales and sales management for over 30 years and has delivered training to over 10,000 professionals over the past 11 years with his own training firm focused on sales and customer service. In his book you will learn about the four personality styles and how each style makes decisions, how they prefer to communicate and what makes them connect with you. Stu addresses how to build a winning sales team, how to lead and how each style prefers to buy.

I've read many books over the course of my career. I have always preferred books that made me change the way I interact with individuals and my teams. I like a book that impacts my behavior as soon as I put it down and not one that I put on the shelf and forget. This book is a game changer. It is the type of read that you will go back to over and over again.

Stu's personality assessment will help you connect or reconnect with individuals and teams so that you can overachieve your goals. I promise that once you finish this book, you will begin to look at people in a totally different light, but most importantly, you will look at yourself differently. It will add a new dimension to how you view others. It will give you a system that you can apply and not always rely on your gut.

Who would've ever imagined that Stu and I would connect on more than having the same shoe size. If we have learned how to connect, this book will help you connect with anyone!
Four People You Should Know is a must read for anyone who has to interact one on one, with two or ten or even 100 people in an organization.

Scott Schlackman

President – Scott Schlackman Global Consulting
Former President – Avon Products, United Kingdom, Continental Europe, Canada, France and Greece
Board of Directors - Medifast

PART 1. INTRODUCTION TO PERSONALITY

1. INTRODUCTION

Dr. Michael Cox, Vice President and Chief Economist of the Dallas Federal Reserve Bank gave an excellent presentation in January 2006 on his research into the skills most needed in the US today. He told the audience:

- The **6th** most needed skill is muscle power.
- **5th** is dexterity
- **4th**, formulaic intelligence
- **3rd**, analytical capability
- **2nd**, creativity.

The **number one** needed skill set needed today is **people skills and emotional intelligence** – a range of skills not taught formally in school, but learned through the experiences we have in life. We can improve our people skills and emotional intelligence by understanding the personality styles of those we associate with on a day-to-day basis.

If we can identify the personality style of those we associate with, we have a much better ability to connect with them from their perspective. If we can view a situation, a sale, a negotiation or a team project through *their* eyes, the chances of success grow exponentially whether you're talking about sales numbers, team productivity or improving customer service. We need to change our view of people from being *difficult* to being *different*. This will open up a whole new dimension as to how we view others.

This book provides an introduction to personality styles, and aims to help you *apply* your new understanding of the personality styles to achieve results in the practical world of selling and other areas such as team building and customer service which require interaction with others daily.

Our personality tool has been developed by taking the best of all the other tools that are available. The Connecting 4 People assessment is only 10 questions but categorizes the four main personality styles quite accurately. You will be able to self-administer the assessment and in a short time you will gain an understanding of your own specific personality color sequence. In parts 3 and 4 of the book I help you gain an understanding of how to leverage this new knowledge of your personality traits *and those of the other personalities.* Specifically, you will learn how to select, from a range of sales strategies and tactics available to you, those that best serve your goals in working with each of the four personality types. We'll look at how to work with each personality in sales situations, with you as the seller gaining a new understanding of your customer. We also explore the dual roles of leadership and contributor, seeing how the use of *personality knowledge* can help maximize sales team performance.

I have used these methods for achieving new levels of sales success and to improve team performance. I teach this system to thousands of salespeople and consultants, helping them improve their chances of success. For me this is not just another theoretical sales tool. Instead it has become an important part of my life, an inner dialog that guides my interactions with clients and colleagues. Every day, I am fortunate to be able to help people learn these approaches.

We will explore many key elements of interacting with others – whether it's in professional or personal situations. We will look at how each personality makes decisions, especially buying decisions. We will examine the different personalities' attitudes and behavior with respect to change, conflict, risk, communication, values and other important matters, and consider how you should use these insights in your sales life, and in your personal life.

The goal in this book is to help you acquire a new skill set – the ability to apply a knowledge of personality styles to your everyday interactions with each of these four different

4

personality types. This will greatly improve your ability to sell and believe it or not everyone is in sales! Selling at the most basic level is the transfer of emotions from one person to another. You are conveying an opinion or an idea to someone else, and want them to accept your point of view. We hope you enjoy discovering more about yourself, and more about others – their preferences, values and needs in life.

2. ABOUT PERSONALITY AND PERSONALITY STYLES

Everyone is different

Exactly what is personality? Psychologists tell us that the foundation of personality is with us from birth. It is part of how we were uniquely made. However, it is also colored by all the experiences we have had. No one else has exactly the same personality and no one else matches our exact perspective on how we view life and respond to its events. Our nature is uniquely made up. Each of us has a different view of life, and each of us responds differently to events and circumstances.

While each of us is unique, we also share distinct similarities with some others. People's personalities can be categorized in broad groupings – personality styles. Understanding those personality styles provides us with insights into the differences and similarities in attitude, preferences and behavior displayed by the people we encounter.

Different personality types tend to communicate differently; to have different values and to make decisions in different ways; to respond in different ways to risk, stress, conflict and change; to learn and teach in subtly different ways; to choose different ways to relax; and to have different preferences for their working environment.

Think for a minute about your own attitudes and preferences, and how they are the same as those of some people you know, and yet quite different from others.

Different people **communicate** differently. Are your conversations filled with small talk and socializing or are they right to the point? Is there a logical flow to your conversation aimed at communicating a specific purpose, or do you express what is on your mind at the moment? Do you tend to debate, fielding and delivering tough questions, or do you just take the conversation in? Do you prefer discussions and meetings with a clear agenda or meetings called at the spur of the moment as needed? Do you prefer to do the talking or the listening?

Critical to making sales and building winning teams, consider how personality reflects what each person **values**. Do you look for the best bang for the buck, or for quality at any price? Is integrity more or less important than results? Is winning the most important thing in life? Or, is having lots of deep friendships the thing to aim for?

Do you **make decisions** impulsively or with deliberation? Do you prefer to make a decision based on logic and judgment or do you make the decision from your heart and emotions? Perhaps you make the decision from the gut on the spur of the moment? Do you consider all the data at hand and continue to ask questions to gather more information while others are perfectly satisfied with the facts before them?

Different personalities also view **risk** differently. Are you extremely cautious or inclined to take a chance? Do you avoid situations where you will face challenges, or seek them out?

People of different personality types vary in how they handle **conflict**. Do you retreat from conflict, avoiding friction? Or do you try to resolve conflict by attacking it head on? Do you find conflict a stimulus to dialog and relationship-building or something that destroys relationships? Or perhaps you just don't see why there is a conflict in the first place. Perhaps you don't know how to handle conflict, and are totally frustrated by it.

Stress can adversely affect health, and how we deal with it has much to do with personality. Do you feel stress when you take on too much responsibility, or when you don't have enough power to control the situation? What makes you more anxious: too much information, or lack of data? Is it more stressful to miss your sales quota or to let down a customer?

More stressful to have an argument or bottle up your emotions?

Each personality views **change** differently. Do you find change invigorating and exciting? Or bothersome, inconvenient and upsetting? Do you like to keep things stable and predictable, or do you enjoy the excitement and stimulus of the new?

When **learning**, do you prefer a lecture environment with traditional testing or do you prefer experiential learning where you advance through trial and error? Do you learn more effectively through hands-on activity or reading about it? When you instruct others what is your preferred method of instruction? Do you lead with theory and process, or simply show them how it's done?

When you **relax**, do you prefer time alone to charge up and re-energize or do you prefer the company of friends and family? Perhaps you have a competitive nature and love games and sports? Or do you prefer working in the garden, watching movies with friends, or quietly reading a book? When you take a vacation, do you organize each day with scheduled events or do you just take each day as it comes, enjoying the excitement of the moment, the spontaneity?

What kind of **working environment** is best for you? Do you prefer to work alone or around others? Do you enjoy interaction? Do you seek a fast paced environment or one that is quiet and orderly? Are you more task-oriented or more relationship focused? What type of **job** attracts you? Do you look for excitement, intellectual stimulus, warm working relationships or satisfaction in achievement? Something else? Do you need a job that demands neatness and order, or do you flourish when you have to handle the unexpected all the time and make spur of the moment decisions?

Answers to these questions tell you a lot about your personality.

The Payoff – Why it's worth making the effort to understand personality

If you can accurately identify someone's personality style you will increase your chances of understanding how they view the world, how they perceive you, and how they will interpret your words and actions. This is true whether it's in a sales situation, a difficult team meeting, or a critical personal situation. You will gain insights into how others make decisions; in what environment they work most effectively; the type of communication that gets through best; how they will react in stressful situations or when conflict arises; and what they find of value to them personally or for their organization. Identifying and understanding personality styles can give you a great advantage in building a relationship with someone – built on *their* terms and not yours.

Your understanding of what's important to them and their needs will set you apart from others who are trying to accomplish the same objectives. It's as if you already know, better than anyone else, how the situation will unfold and how the story will end.

It's fairly simple for a sales person to ask the customer: 'what are your needs?' But sometimes a sales person can gather all the information, use it intelligently to present an appropriate solution, accurately convey the value of the solution – but still not win the sale. Why not? Usually we come to the conclusion that the competition was more aggressive, came up with a better price/performance package, or had better products. Sometimes we never find out the real reason.

Understanding personality styles helps us to gain further insights into why people make one buying decision rather than another. People make decisions based on two distinct sets of needs: personal needs and business needs. Business needs are logical and objective, emotional needs are personal and subjective.

10

Both are important, yet often a sales person undervalues one or the other. A sales person who is strong on relationships will be successful with a customer of similar temperament, but might underestimate the importance of performance data to a customer that needs the reassurance of facts. A sales person who is very data-oriented may not make due allowance for the way the customer *feels* about the deal.

Emotional needs are complex and have strong effects. Some examples of emotional needs are:

- Caring how you perceive that others will view you: for example, weighing what others within your company will think of you if you make a decision one way or another.

- Having a driving quest for a promotion, a raise, a bonus or a power play within the organization, rather than doing what is best for the company.

These personal needs will impact buying decisions. Sometimes, what appears on the surface as an objective, measurable business need, becomes subjective at the time a buying decision must be made. The answers to questions such as 'How will this decision impact employee morale?' 'How will it affect our competitive position?' or 'What will our customer think of this?' are subject to emotional, personal perspectives that vary for specific personality types. Here, the buyer perceives the impact of the buying decision as a personal impact on them or their colleagues. Often the buying decision-maker will not reveal emotional needs until the seller has built up a relationship with this person.

Business needs are not as hard to determine since they are generally logical and codified into a company's measurements for success. Customers can quantify the value of business needs. They can weigh how a purchase or decision will impact productivity, revenue, expenses, research and development, and market share. For some customers such business perspectives dominate the decision-making process, with emotional factors in the background. For others, the emotion can dominate, with business factors only taken into account to establish minimum objective requirements.

When you understand a customer's personality style, you are more able to determine, in any specific case, whether the personal needs are more important than the business needs, or visa versa. Is Mary more objective or subjective? Will John look for only the tangible benefits or the intangible ones also? Will their decisions focus more on the quantitative aspects or the qualitative?

When I'm the buyer, the sales person had better build a relationship with me or I'll walk out the door. For my personality type, the act of selecting a car, for example, is personal and my emotions will lead. But in selecting a dealer and negotiating a price, I compete hard. My personality style is to make everything into a competition.

However, when I'm the seller, I would never win a sale negotiating in my typical competitive style. When I'm in a business situation selling a customer a product, I know that I have to work with their personality and adjust my behavior to meet the needs of their personality style. My knowing the customer's personality style will change the strategy and tactics I use to influence the buying decision.

For example, if the customer is a conservative person, cautious and data-oriented, I will try to provide objective facts and figures with realistic estimates of payback and return on investment. Trying to get that type of customer excited about the impact on public image or employee morale might not work so well.

On the other hand, a different personality type might lose interest when being led through the details and analysis of how the product or service might work. For someone competitive and ambitious, it might pay off more to focus on how the solution will win new business, and maybe improve the way he or she is viewed in the organization.

Understanding someone's personality will help you tailor your strategy and guide your approach when influencing him or her to take specific actions. It will help you understand what drives their ego. A tailored strategy will vary for each personality and reflect the circumstances around the decision that needs to be made. I have found that, too often, personality is the dimension that is missing in the sales approach.

Personality models

For at least two millennia, possibly beginning with Hippocrates in 370 BC, the concept of personality has intrigued people. Most of these approaches lead up to the 'psychological types' of Carl Jung (1875-1961), codified and used by Myers-Briggs. But the real breakthrough came in modern times when the Minnesota Multiphasic Personality Inventory (MMPI) applied matching and grouping statistics to objective tests.

There are many excellent personality tools available today. Answers to seemingly random questions can be correlated to known personality disorders and then turned around and given to new subjects, becoming a predictive tool in classifying them. Originally developed for aiding clinical diagnosis, this same approach can also classify healthy individuals by personality type. There are many personality tools that can be used to help the individual understand more about their own inclination and how they view life. Besides MMPI & Myers-Briggs, there are DISC, Brainstyles, Insight Learning Foundation, David Keirsey, the Four Social Styles and many others.

Each of these approaches assesses a number of personality characteristics, and combines the findings to classify the subject as a personality type. For example,

13

assessment questions will probe:

- what you value,
- what motivates you,
- how you view risk and conflict,
- how you make decisions,
- how you communicate,
- how you respond to change.

These tests and classifications help you understand your strengths and weaknesses, your ability to cope with daily circumstances, and will help you be attuned to those around you. You will be more aware of why people behave the way the do.

While we must be careful in our generalizations, to the extent these methods are rigorously, scientifically, correlated with known behaviors, they are accurate predictors of those observed personality characteristics. Each of the models developed over the years has its strengths. Some are more suitable for academic use, others for clinical purposes.

Some, like Myers-Briggs, have strong clinical applications, but with sixteen different classified personality measures, are rather complex for daily use. Some other systems have simplified to four or five groups. Furthermore, these personality tools alone don't teach you how to *apply* their results toward facilitating your interactions with personalities different from your own.

The Connecting 4 People assessment is practical for business purposes. It is a powerful yet simple tool, but can readily be applied by non-psychologists to gain useful and applicable insights.

3.   INTRODUCING THE CONNECTING 4 PEOPLE ASSESSMENT

After many years in the sales business, I grew more and more convinced that we were missing a big opportunity to make our approach to sales more effective. The gap was that many sales people lacked an understanding of the personality factors that influence the course of the sales relationship and affect buying decisions.

I am the sort of person that finds it really easy to relate to others. At the same time, I am pretty good at establishing the objective needs of the customer and pitching the logically correct solution. Usually this helps me to bond with my customer, build a relationship and move the deal towards a successful close. However, I found that sometimes this approach just did not work.

Why did my formula work in some cases and not at all in others?

One time, as I engaged the client with small talk, he made an impatient grimace. I took this as a signal to get down to business. At that point I asked the business questions I'd planned and the answers I received were short and succinct – almost curt, from my perception.

As the conversation continued the client asked me very detailed questions about our services. I saw this as a test. My gut reaction was that he was trying to stump me. I became defensive. I became anxious as I formed the impression that the customer was not feeling at all positive about our offerings, our company – or me.

Today, I can see that my understanding of that sales-customer relationship was way off track. Let's dive back into that moment and see why. As the salesperson, I had developed a perception of the client as challenging and distrustful. I'd stopped believing that we would win the business and my behavior reflected this. Because I became defensive, every decision I made was made with doubt, not with confidence. It's hard to win when you play defensively.

Another example. On one occasion, competing for a sale against IBM, I really thought I had won the deal. I was sure I had the better solution and the better value proposition, so I was dismayed when the decision went to the competition. I had focused on objective facts and logic, while the IBM sales person had established a high level personal relationship that gave the customer a lot of reassurance – a strong emotional pull in favor of the IBM solution.

Meeting emotional needs is often just as important as delivering the logical requirements of the solution. Sometimes people will buy the more expensive solution to meet their emotional needs! The sales people at IBM have an exceptional ability to understand what motivates their customers to buy. IBM sales executives are known for getting to the decision makers and building strong relationships. They are excellent at understanding both the logical side and the emotional side of the executive's needs and striking the right balance.

In the first example, I missed the target because I focused too much on the relationship factors, and misinterpreted the customer's need for hard facts as hostility. I assumed I was dealing with someone like myself, someone who viewed the world in much the same way is I did. In the second example I focused on facts and completely missed the need for building a strong high-level relationship!

I soon realized I was projecting my own thought processes on to my perception of the customer. I needed to learn how to change my approach to include a real understanding of the personality of the customer, and modify

16

my own natural approach to match both the needs of the customer, as well as the nature of the solution.

To do this, I felt that we needed an easy-to-use, practical, yet accurate tool to help understand our daily interactions. After researching many of the personality tools, myself and my brother Scott created the "Connecting 4 People" assessment so anyone can apply the information in any business setting. The tool uses four colors (Blue, Gold, Green and Orange) as easy mnemonics for remembering personality groups.

Why is this system so effective for every day use? First, with colors, it's easy to remember and identify the characteristics of each of the four personalities. It's easy to add the color to the details we remember about the many people we meet such as their face, name, and workplace, thereby remembering that person's personality style.

In this book, the focus is not only on who you are, but who the other person is and how that person's personality affects behavior. We focus on how to apply the concepts to create effective communications with the other personality styles, when you're:

- selling to a client;
- building or strengthening a versatile team;
- leading a team;
- or being involved in personal situations and day-to-day business interactions.

I describe ways to ensure effective communications with each type of personality. We teach you how to *color* your communications to achieve your objective - connecting with different personalities and understanding what is important to them. This book is about learning about others, and understanding to their perspectives.

Parts 3 and 4 will help you understand how to apply the information from the assessment in Part 2 where I describe the four main personality styles – Blue, Gold, Green and Orange.

You should take the assessment and discover your own color sequence. Check your characteristics against those described for your primary color type. Give the assessment to a few friends and compare their color classifications against your experience with them. This will give you trust and familiarity with the Connecting 4 People system. This will establish the foundation for the rest of the book, which will help you understand how to apply personality to selling, customer service and working with teams.

Part 2. The Connecting 4 People Assessment

Taking the Assessment

Discovering the characteristics of your personality is the first step in understanding your temperament. We all have all four colors, but it's the order that makes you unique.

This assessment will identify your sequence. It questions addressed cover the following ten categories:

- Decisions,
- Relating to others,
- Frustration,
- Value at work,
- Conflict,
- Learning,
- Communication,
- Motivation,
- Expression,
- Making a purchase.

Read the sentence and the four possible endings. Compare each ending to the other three. Then determine how much each ending describes you. **Put the endings in order.** Write a **4** beside the one that is most like you, a **3** beside the one that is next most like you, a **2** beside the one that is next, and a **1** beside the one that is least like you. Repeat this step until all ten categories have been scored.

Most like me: 4 points

More like me: 3 points

Less like me: 2 points

Least like me: 1 point

You must be honest to make sure your results will be as accurate as possible. Don't answer the way you think you are or how other people think you should be. Don't answer the way you wish you were or would like to be—answer honestly the way you really are. This assessment is geared towards your work environment, but also describes your behaviors outside of work. Each question is ranked so a number cannot be used twice.

You will notice the letters used to answer each question spell TEAM. There is a reason for that. It describes one attribute of each of the personality styles as you will see throughout the book. Each of the letters in TEAM represent a color.

Don't get too deep into the question. Go by your first reaction to the question. It should take around ten minutes. When you're done go to the Score Sheet that follows.

Good luck!

4. The Connecting 4 People Assessment

1. DECISIONS

I typically make decisions based on:

_____   E. Research and analysis.

_____   M. Practicality and gut feel.

_____   A. A checklist and process to evaluate.

_____   T. Trust and consensus.

2. RELATING TO OTHERS

I relate best to people that are:

_____   M. Energetic and upbeat.

_____   A. Loyal and reliable.

_____   T. Open and friendly
.
_____   E. Curious and knowledgeable.

3. FRUSTRATION

It bothers me when:

_____ E. Others just ramble on for no reason.

_____ M. There is too much unnecessary detail.

_____ A. People are late and unprepared.

_____ T. People are insincere.

4. VALUE AT WORK

As part of a team I value:

_____ M. Results and action.

_____ A. Follow through and structure

_____ T. Harmony and cooperation

_____ E. Efficiency and ingenuity.

5. CONFLICT

When there is conflict I tend to:

_____ E. Address it with the facts unemotionally.

_____ M. Get right to the point.

_____ A. Approach it with preparation.

_____ T. Avoid it if at all possible.

6. LEARNING

I learn best when:

_____ M. I do things hands on by trial and error.

_____ A. I use process and methods.

_____ T. I'm interactive in a group setting.

_____ E. I use discovery and experimentation.

7. COMMUNICATION

I prefer communication that is:

_____ E. Succinct and inquisitive.

_____ M. Fast paced with stories and analogies.

_____ A. Direct and proper
.

_____ T. Sincere and open.

8. MOTIVATION

I am motivated when recognized for:

_____ M. My performance and talent.

_____ A. Planning and dependability.

_____ T. Creativity and contribution.

_____ E. Expertise and new ideas.

26

9. EXPRESSION

I express myself by being:

_____ E. Calm and can be skeptical.

_____ M. Animated and convincing.

_____ A. Controlled and confident.

_____ T. Pleasant and obliging.

10. BUYING

I typically make a buying decision when:

_____ M. I see immediate benefits and it's a good deal.

_____ A. It's justified and meets a need.

_____ T. It feels right and others agree.

_____ E. I've done my research and it's the best choice.

Score Sheet

To find your personality sequence add the scores for each of the letters. There are 10 scores for each letter and the total should be 100 when you add all the scores together.

Scores	Color	Color	Rank
T=Trust	Turquoise Blue		
E=Expertise	Evergreen Green		
A=Accountability	Amber Gold		
M=Momentum	Mandarin Orange		

The acronym TEAM gives one main characteristic of that personality style. For example, T-Turquoise Blue is about Trust, E-Evergreen Green is about Expertise, a-Amber Gold is about Accountability and M- Mandarin Orange is about Momentum

For simplicity moving forward we will use just the colors Blue, Green, Gold and Orange.

1st   Your dominant personality style

_____

2nd   Your second style does influence you

_____

3rd   Not much influence unless close to second score

_____

4th   Your lowest - least like you

_____

Your sequence tells you what you prefer most (your highest score) and what you dislike or least care about (your

28

lowest score). If all your scores are close it means you can relate to each personality a little easier than if they are far apart. Having a high dominant score means you are stronger in the characteristics of that color and if your lowest score is quite low, it's something you don't really care about and can be considered a weakness. No combination of scores and sequence is better than others. It's understanding who you are and how to leverage your strengths, understand and minimize your weaknesses that matters most.

Understanding the characteristics of you color sequence is the beginning to understanding yourself and how you interact with the other colors. My brother Scott and I have taken this concept to a whole new level by developing programs to reinforce what you gain from this book. Whether it's a keynote or a half-day seminar, we will help you better understand how to become a world class team.

Visit our website at www.connecting4people.com to view our in-depth offerings and support materials.

5. THE BLUE PERSONALITY

The Blue personality type is your amiable personality type. They are all about "people and passion." Their goal is to get along with others. In the Myers-Briggs model they are your intuitive feelers. They look for the deeper meaning in life. Understanding who they are and how they can make a difference is important to the Blue. Blues want to make an impact in society. They want to make contributions and they want to be recognized for them.

A good example of a Blue making an impact on society is our son Bryan. Back when he graduated college he went on a trip to Europe with the goal of raising funds for water purification systems for Africa. Bryan walked from Northern Ireland to Valencia, Spain. Blues love to get involved in causes that can make an impact on society.

Blues value honesty and trust. Blues will not make a commitment or a purchase if they do not feel the other person is sincere. They like to have small talk to get to know you on the personal side, not just the business. Maintaining eye contact with a Blue is important since lacking the connection can cause suspicion.

Blues are good listeners and therefore tend to ask questions which are focused on the other person and getting to know who they truly are. For this, Blues easily open up and share emotions and typically are transparent with others and look for the same in return. They are good communicators and are very aware of gestures and mannerisms.

Blues want everything to be in harmony and for teammates to get along. They dislike conflict and will typically avoid it. If Blues have been hurt in the past, their memory has a hard time letting go of it. It can seem like it happened just yesterday. My brother Scott is the perfect example of a Blue. With two kids at college age, a three-year-old and one on the way, Scott needs his space. His way of calming down is to go for a nice long, long walk to keep his balance and gain harmony.

Relationships are what Blues value the most. Whether it's family, friends or coworkers they thrive on being with people. Blues have lifelong friends and staying in touch and getting together for any occasion is what makes them thrive. One of my best friends in life, Mike Nader is a Blue personality. Every time Mike has come to visit us, we received a thank you card several days later. This is typical of the Blue personality. The thank you card is not just a card saying thanks, it's a card that recaps the entire experience of being with us day to day, and reminiscing what he thought was special. Mike is a true Blue. In fact, with Blues if you don't stay in touch they might think something is wrong. But for me, an Orange, it's not that I purposely not stay in touch, it's that it's not at the top of my mind like a Blue.

Blues are usually optimistic and they are patient. It takes more than the other personalities to frustrate and upset a Blue. Blues are your steady personality that can go along without making any drastic decisions or changes. In fact, Blues look at change as disruptive most of the time since they like things consistent and predictable.

Blues are the most creative of the styles since creativity is in their quadrant of the brain. They thrive in a brainstorming type situation. Since they have a creative flair they will gravitate to the arts and literature such as poetry.

When it comes to making decisions, Blues take their time since making the right decision is important. It's based on feeling more so than logic, therefore there is no rush. Also, consensus is important to the Blue. If they are going to go out to purchase a car it becomes a family event. A Blue would not make a purchase unless the family agreed with it. Also, if a sales person is pushy with the Blue, the sales experience is

32

over. Blues do not like to be pressured or forced into a decision. It has to happen on their timeframe.

When a Blue is in a sales career their success is based on the relationships they develop. Their strength is in building trust, loyalty and selling themselves first. For a customer, what impacts them the most about the Blue is their likeability factor and that they are responsive, since strong relationships is the top priority. Since Blues are patient with customers, they tend to focus on pleasing the customer whenever possible.

Blues have a win-win attitude with customers and teammates. Making sure that all are satisfied is important. This is because of the empathy that Blues often have for others. Especially those they are closest to. Blues will adapt to make sure others are pleased.

Blues also tend to avoid risk especially around others. Safety is an important factor for them. If the speed limit on a highway says 65 miles per hour, there is a strong chance that the will follow accordingly. They will also avoid risk when it comes to financial investments, since taking care of their family long term is of great importance.

When it comes to careers Blues gravitate to positions that are creative and those that require patience. Blues make excellent teachers for the elementary school's years since they are nurturing. They also do well in human resources, counseling, social work, nursing, insurance and real estate agents, advertising and other areas that require high touch with people and relationships. Blues also do a lot of nonprofit work and charity since they are keen to get involved in causes they are passionate about.

It is rare to have a Blue in a high stress job. A job that requires numerous deadlines and conflict within other departments does not sit well with the Blue. What's important to a Blue when they join a company is their mission, vision and values. Blues thrive in customer service positions since they enjoy pleasing and satisfying the needs of others.

Blues enjoy getting positive reinforcement and feedback for a job well done. If this is lacking they can become frustrated and disappointed. They want to make sure that their thoughts and ideas are recognized and supported by those around them. They thrive on being appreciated.

When Blues believe in something they are all in. Whether it's a job, a cause or volunteering, what matters the most to the Blue is impacting the lives of those around them. They can become intense about what they believe in and can spend too much time in accomplishing what matters most to them. The Blue needs to find the meaning in each of their endeavors.

The Blue personality is the glue to the team. Since harmony and cooperation are important they will be proactive in making sure all is running smoothly on the team. If a new member joins the team, it's typically the Blues that will welcome them into the fold. You have to have Blues on your team.

6. THE GOLD PERSONALITY

The Gold personality can be best described as a driver. They are the get it done personality. They are about process and planning. In Myers-Briggs they are known as sensory judgers. Golds value order and one of their greatest strengths is their organization skills. Golds immediately take control to put things in the right order. They make rules to make sure everything functions orderly. They will turn chaos into clarity at all cost.

Golds prioritize duty and service and many times are driven to do things out of obligation. It's the right thing to do. Golds commonly volunteer their time for service in areas such as watch patrols for their community, and other groups that service a city. My good friend Todd who is a Gold, puts together the schedule for our watch patrol not because he was asked to, but because it has to be done and the Gold will be the one to step up and be proactive.

Golds believe that everyone should be responsible. They are strong initiators of projects, activities, organizing and gets things accomplished. Golds are more about giving than receiving and that gives them a sense of self-worth. They believe in discipline, follow through and that everyone should do their share of the work.

Golds are very good with money. They understand its value and always evaluate whether or not something should be purchased. There needs to be a reason to buy something and a Gold will always measure the return on investment. They will evaluate the pros and cons before making any decision.

You can tell a Gold personality by looking at their bedroom closet. This gives you an excellent understanding of how they organize. Everything is always in its proper place. Shoes are organized. Shirts of the same style will be in the same section as well as pants, suits, etc. In fact, all clothes will be facing in the same direction and even the hangers will be facing the same way. This is the opposite of me, the Orange personality where you might trip and fall in my closet. There is no organization in my closet. I have more hooks with shirts and pants hanging that can change on a day to day basis.

The Gold personality sees things as predictable and consistent. There is always the right way to do things and if it's not done right it shouldn't be done at all. Golds get right to the point and are black or white on their opinions and views.

Golds can actually become compulsive about being orderly and having a routine. If things are messy, they will automatically start cleaning things up. We have one good friend that is a Gold and you can tell just by taking a peak of her kitchen pantry. You know they're a Gold when their Campbell Soup cans are in alphabetical order!

Golds also desire punctuality and get frustrated when someone is late to a meeting. I conducted a seminar at Ebby Halliday and one of the participants asked me when the seminar would be ending. He was a Gold and I told him we would be done at noon. Exactly at noon he got up and left. The seminar ended at three minutes after twelve, but he couldn't wait. Golds expect you to meet your commitments and deadlines. I have another good friend that I used to go jogging with. One time I was five minutes late and he already starting jogging without me. I asked him why he didn't wait for me and he said it was 5:30 pm which was our scheduled time to start. I just scratched my head since as an Orange I was more interested in the time together than starting on time.

Not only do Golds schedule their lives but they are fanatical about following their to-do list. At the end of the day they feel good when the achieved everything they set out to get done for the day. If their schedule gets disrupted it can be highly frustrating. When meetings are canceled or moved around, it can ruin their day since they had in mind what they

36

wanted to accomplish before the day even started. The reason for this is because Golds measure everything so they can feel good about their accomplishments. That's why the best project managers in companies are typically Golds. The mantra is "on time- on budget."

Golds believe in action steps and actions plans. They believe in using Robert's Rules of Order for meetings. A meeting is a waste of time in their view if there is no agenda. Everyone needs to know the reason for the meeting and what will be accomplished. There must be action items from meetings and who will take ownership of them.

Golds are the ones that create the rules in society. If they walk into a situation that is lacking clarity on who does what or what steps should be taken in a process, the Gold will take control and set the rules and expectations for the operation of that specific business process. Breaking or not following the rules is highly frustrating for the Gold personality.

Golds are excellent for planning for the future when it comes to investments, purchases and taking care of their household. They are very good about saving for a rainy day and want to make sure all is protected just in case something goes wrong. They tend to be pessimistic due to the mindset of looking at what might go wrong. Myself as an Orange being optimistic doesn't even think something might go wrong. Even more so since my lowest personality style is Gold.

Golds gravitate to clubs and organizations sometime just to have the sense of belonging and that it's the right thing to do. My good friend Glen who's a Gold was president of our high school class all three years and belonged to several groups that supported the student body. For Glen it was the right thing to do.

Golds always put work before play. That is the responsible thing to do. I wish I can say the same as an Orange, but if an opportunity to play golf comes along, I just might rearrange my schedule. Of course, as an Orange I don't always have a schedule so that's easy.

Golds are very predictable on getting things done when they're committed to a deadline. This is a top priority since it has to do with their work ethic and making and keeping commitments. Breaking a commitment is unacceptable and unprofessional.

Golds are traditional and as they get older they become more of who they are. You will see that Golds want things to go a certain way with holidays and traditions each year. Whether it's Thanksgiving, Christmas or another event such as an anniversary, Golds put high value on family gatherings and other events.

Golds like Blues see change as disruptive most of the time. They like to see things running smoothly without any glitches. In other words, if it ain't broke, don't fix it.

You can rely on the Gold personality since they are dedicated to the organization and its goals. They will get things done whether or not they have support. Golds will take the initiative when others are hesitant. They pride themselves in being responsible.

Golds rise in the areas of leadership and management. It's a natural progression for them since they are interested in accomplishing the good of the organization and all involved. A majority of CEO's fall into the Gold personality. Golds do well in careers in education at the higher level, lawyers, banking and investments, the military because it has rank and administrative positions that need a high degree of organization skills.

Golds create the rules where Oranges typically break the rules. Golds ask permission where Oranges ask forgiveness. Golds enjoy being in charge and having control. This way they can navigate and define the order and rules that they think suit everyone the best.

When it comes to sales, Golds are best at selling the company where Blues sell themselves. They understand the benefits of their products and services. Gold customers want to do business with companies that are stable and have a successful track record. Stability, structure, organization and order is what Golds value the most.

Golds bring consistency and stability to your team. They are the workhorse that makes sure everyone is doing their share and goals are getting accomplished. You need to have Golds on your team.

7. THE GREEN PERSONALITY

The Green personality is the new ideas person. They are your analytical type and they are all about perfection and precision. They are the get it right person. In Myers-Briggs they are intuitive thinkers. For the Green logic trumps emotion. It's Spock in the old Star Trek series. Always thinking of new ways to do things, problem solving and always having the response "have you thought about doing it this way?"

Greens love to learn. For them knowledge is power. The more they learn the better they feel. You don't have to tell a Green to read a book and learn something new. That's their natural wiring. They thrive on logic and reason which is their natural strength.

A great example of this is my good friend Trevor Hayes. Several years ago we went on one of our Dallas Ski Club trips to Aspen. Trevor was still fairly new at skiing and thought his best method of improvement would be to purchase a book on skiing. This is quite typical for a Green and totally illogical for me, an Orange. What can a book teach? The book explained gravity and how to approach the slope. Trevor's saying was "gravity is my friend." Today he is an outstanding skier and he always refers back to the book.

Greens are lifetime learners. Just ask my good friend and pastor Hank Lamb who reads over 80 books a year and of course is a Green. Being the most competent at their trade is a priority. The greatest strength of a Green is their expertise. For the Green the means is "performance" and the end result is "ability." They are driven to improve and they will research and practice until they have arrived at perfection.

Greens are extremely innovative. Take a look at a company like Apple or Google where innovation is the focus of the company. A majority of the people at these companies are the Green personality. In fact, Google gives their

41

employees a creativity day to go off and create new ideas or new projects to improve a product or a service. Greens love their freedom to just go off and do.

Greens like to tinker with things and experiment. If they are into something that is intriguing they can do it for hours and hours. For the Green work is more like a hobby. Experimentation is something that comes automatic. When a new software application comes out the curiosity of Green makes them the first to learn it and use it. It's like my good friend Don Jones who's Green and self-taught himself how to use PowerPoint many years ago. I was amazed at all the charts and graphics he was able to imbed in his slides. As an Orange I just wanted to figure out how to add a new slide into the presentation. Greens don't need any help figuring things out.

Greens are not too keen on rules. Golds typically make the rules and Greens question the rules. Rules from the Green's perspective restricts their freedom. If you ask them to figure something out, having a set of rules is not part of their thought process. The goal of the Green is perfection and it will be done at all costs.

Many years ago when I was working at Digital Equipment Corporation we had an award ceremony at the end of the year called DEC 100 for making 100% of your annual budget. At the time I was working for Don Jones my longtime friend and mentor. Several years earlier the award for DEC 100 was a four-day cruise to the Bahamas. As times got lean it became a one night stay in Fort Worth. Not too exciting if you lived in Dallas or Austin. The year after the event in Fort Worth, Don figured out how to get DEC 100 to be a four-day event in Martha's Vineyard. He figured if he combined a little training with the event it would be justified. He pulled it off and I couldn't believe it! Only a Green would figure that out.

You can identify someone who's Green just by listening to the many different things they know. They are constantly reading, learning and watching educational videos while no

42

one is looking. Greens are typically introverted and enjoy their alone time to re-energize and do their research.

Besides pushing to increase their knowledge Greens will challenge others to do the same. They want others to observe learn and discover what they have learned. You can identify two Greens in a discussion when they go from one intellectual topic to another. It's like watching a game of ping pong. They also love to debate each other since Greens are also your biggest skeptics.

Because Greens thrive on information and love to learn, they are incredible at researching when looking to buy something. Typically, they will explore on the internet what they're looking to purchase and by the time they get to the store, they know more about the product than the sales person.

Green customers are your toughest. They ask many tough questions, come across skeptical and you never know where you stand. Since they need so much information to come to a decision, they are slow in committing. They must have all the facts, statistics and what the competition offers. A sales person can become highly frustrated unless they understand they are working with a Green personality. Never push the Green to closure or make them look ignorant. You will lose any chance of making a sale.

When it comes to communication with a Green, make your point. Stay away from small talk since that gets in the way of the information they are looking for. Greens prefer succinct communication. Like my good friend Rick Huskisson says, "skip the adjectives and just give me the nouns." Well said by a true Green personality.

The best way to understand the Green personality on a sales call is to be prepared with questions that get them to open up. Green like to play their cards close to the vest, not giving you any idea of where you might stand with them on moving the sale forward. It typically takes the longest to get the commitment from a Green.

Rarely will you see a Green get emotional. They are typically soft spoken, patient and do not like to be the center of attention. They prefer the side lines and get involved when they see a good intellectual discussion or debate forming.

Greens prefer their alone time, so when a party or gathering comes up they don't usually get excited. When at a gathering they will seek out a close friend and might engage in a lengthy discussion that will occupy the time. They are not anti-sociable, but prefer one on one instead of a large crowd.

Since Greens are avid learners and enjoy detail, it's common for them to have a career in the sciences. Disciplines like information technology, science, engineering, medicine and dentistry and naturals for a Green. Their eye for detail, research and innovation makes the Green so valuable to society. Just look at a Steve Jobs with Apple or Bill Gates with Microsoft. They are excellent examples of your Green personality.

Greens are always envisioning the future and the "what can be." If there is a better way to do something it will usually be the Green that figures it out

You need to have a Green on your team. They will enlighten the other members to what the possibilities can be.

44

8. THE ORANGE PERSONALITY

Describing the Orange personality style is an easy one for me since I'm Orange. Where my brother Scott is Blue and is careful and deliberate in what he does, I just barrel forward. The Orange is your expressive personality. They are the get appreciated type. In Myers-Briggs they are sensory perceivers and have great imagination. Oranges can have that 'aha' moment where they connect the dots that a Green personality might have created.

One of the drawbacks of the Orange that I can easily admit to, is that I do not have patience. Just watch me drive. I expect the highway to part like the Red Sea. Just ask my wife Betty who is my best witness. Oranges need momentum. They need to have things moving at a fast pace or they get bored. It's easy to lose the attention of an Orange if something is slow moving, boring or too detailed. Oranges are your big picture people. Just get to the point, help me understand what you're trying to accomplish and let's get to it!

A great example is from my first job out of college. It's hard to believe that as an Orange I have a degree in Mechanical Engineering, which I explain later in the book. My first job was taking off piping and fittings from a blue print for nuclear power plants. My supervisor explained to me what was to be accomplished and then I went about doing the job. Two days later I turned in the project complete which made the entire department upset, since I had two weeks to complete the project, but no one told me that. Yes, Oranges are fast paced because they get bored easily. They might start many different projects and not get them completed. Since I like to be appreciated, I'll focus on getting the job done so I get that pat on the back that I so much enjoy.

Impulsivity is in the Orange quadrant of the brain which causes the impatience, the boredom and spur of the moment decisions. Therefore, Oranges are risk takers, find change exciting and multi-task. In fact, as I'm writing this, I've already taken several breaks this morning to piddle in something else I needed to get done.

Oranges want action and they enjoy their freedom. As an engineer early on I did not enjoy what I was doing. Sitting at a drawing board all day counting pipe fittings for the Extraction Steam system for a Pressurized Water Reactor was not my idea of excitement. Many Oranges will get into the world of sales like I did later on in life because of the many different responsibilities in the sales cycle. I might do some cold calling, prospecting, putting together a solution, present to a client or try to gain commitment. That excites me. Especially working with customers. Oranges enjoy building relationships and are very good at connecting and networking.

One problem Oranges can have is doing too much of the talking. They love to be in the spotlight and be the center of attention. This can lead to smothering a conversation and not gaining enough information from the other person. Oranges think from their own perspective which can be detrimental in a sales situation. Where my brother Scott as a Blue likes to learn about the other person and build a relationship, I will try to do the same and not realize that I might be hogging the conversation and completing the other person's sentence. That doesn't work.

Oranges get excited easily and are the most optimistic of the personality styles. That can lead to unrealistic expectations that might set them up for disappointment. Especially when it comes to my golf game. If my game is going well, I'll start thinking if I par the next three holes I can shoot in the low 80's. Then comes the high risk shot under the tree and over the pond. Instead of laying up to set up an easy shot to the green, I'll take the risk of trying to get over the pond and on the green. So much for being realistic and goodbye low 80's!

Another trait of the Orange is that the means is "ability" and the end result is "performance." That's the opposite of the Green just mentioned. In others words, I don't like to

46

practice. Let's just play golf or when I play tennis there is no reason to practice my serve. Let's just start playing and I'll warm up as we play. It drives my wife Betty crazy.

Oranges live for the moment, it's now that counts and being spontaneous is my mode of operation. Where a Gold might plan each day on a vacation down to each detail, I don't even know the day we're flying out of town. Neither does my wife Betty who is also an Orange. We've actually gone to a wedding on the wrong Saturday and have missed two flights because we showed up a day late. Not good.

Oranges also don't mind crises. Since we are highly competitive and look at everything in life as a game, we take crises as a challenge to conquer them. Problem solving and getting things accomplished is more of a competitive challenge to me than a job. Oranges get excited when faced with a challenge. They also like to shine in the limelight. I asked one insurance sales agent why they enjoy selling and his answer was he likes to make a lot of money and be the hero to his family. That's exactly the Orange's mindset, and yes, Oranges do get excited about the opportunity to make big sales commissions. That can also be a drawback where they might have the wrong focus for doing business and yes, I have to keep myself in check on that.

Oranges are very hands on. As I mentioned they are sensory perceivers in Myers-Briggs. They would rather do something than learn something from a book. In other words, show me how to do it. You will find many Oranges in trades such as carpentry, plumbing, electrical and masonry. Doing a different job every couple of hours, getting into their truck and going the next different job, fits the Orange personality style.

Since Oranges enjoy being the center of attention you will experience hearing many stories from them and maybe even several jokes. Oranges enjoy entertaining others, making them laugh and turning a possible boring time into lots of fun. If they find a function boring, they'll try to spice it up by taking main stage.

Oranges have great stamina and in tough situations are typically the best at weathering the storm. They are resilient when it comes to tough times and facing possible defeat. This is primarily due to their optimism. They are the least of the personality styles to play the victim. Even though I can be serious, most of the time as an Orange I'm light-hearted and jovial.

Oranges are typically the ones to take a challenge first or volunteer. They are bold in their approach and like to jump in head first. Oranges are not afraid to make a mistake, learn from it, correct mid-stream and move on. It's better than planning and trying to do things to perfection. That's the mindset of the Orange.

Oranges usually are attracted to action jobs like sales and marketing. Also, a high percentage of professional speakers are Orange. They love being center stage and getting the attention from others. They love to please the crowd. Oranges make great entrepreneurs since that don't have a problem with risk. High risk-high reward. Oranges make great fighter pilots like Tom Cruise in the movie Top Gun. They also are great at negotiating since to the Orange, it's a game and we must win.

Oranges want action, that's the bottom line. They are the energizer bunny of the team. They'll keep everyone motivated to press on and get the job done. You need an Orange on your team.

9. PERSONALITY RECAP

Here is a summary of some of the key characteristics just explained.

Blues:

- Are focused on people and passion
- Desire harmony
- Relationships are very important
- They enjoy small talk
- Family and friends are a priority
- They are creative and artistic
- They want everyone to get along
- They're intuitive by nature
- They make decisions on emotions and feeling
- They enjoy careers with high interaction with people
- Get involved with charities and causes
- Are friendly and likeable
- Avoid risk
- Make decisions carefully
- Are nurturers
- Are the glue of the team.

With Blues do: Be sincere, maintain eye contact, listen and be encouraging.

With Blues do not: Ignore feelings, pressure them, be controversial or too direct and formal.

Golds:

- Are focused on process and planning
- Drivers to get things done
- Excellent planners
- Great organizers
- Focused on schedules and time
- Loyal and dedicated
- Make and keep commitments
- Traditional by nature
- Plan for the future
- Serious minded
- Bottom line driven
- Agenda driven
- Enjoy being in charge
- Financial focused
- Bring structure and stability to the team.

With Golds do: Be formal and serious, be on point and have an agenda, support the goals and objectives.

With Golds do not: Waste their time, be unprepared, be indecisive or too casual.

Greens:

- Are focused on precision and perfection
- Love to learn
- Are experts at what they do
- Desire freedom to innovate
- Avid readers
- Must have all the information to make a decision
- Want succinct communications
- Are inquisitive
- Logic trumps emotion
- Typically introverted
- Can do things for hours if it's interesting
- Desire technical occupations
- Like to work independently
- Are futuristic
- Bring new ideas to the team.

With Greens do: Know your information, remain factual, focus on process.

With Greens do not: Lack detail, get emotional or have too much small talk.

Oranges:

- Are focused on performance and persuasion
- Will take risks
- Life is a game
- Are optimistic
- Highly competitive
- Take on crises head on
- Are hands on with their occupation
- Enjoy the limelight
- Have perseverance
- Enjoy multi-tasking
- Impulsive on decisions
- Story tellers and enjoy communicating
- Typically extraverted
- Casual by nature
- The energizer bunny of the team.

With Oranges do: Be flexible, have enthusiasm, let them talk.

With Oranges do not: Be too detailed, be rigid, slow paced or serious.

PART 3. EXPLORING PERSONALITY STYLES

10. UNDERSTANDING YOUR OWN PERSONALITY COLOR

First, know yourself

Knowing yourself is the first step. Before you can extend this to knowing others, you must spend some time getting to know yourself. You should also observe the attitudes and behaviors of your friends and work associates, and contrast them with your own attitudes and behavior. You now know what your color spectrum is.

Spend time examining your own strengths and aptitudes, so you can appreciate how they are linked to your color spectrum. Compare yourself to others. How are others different from you? In what ways are you different from others?

It is also important to understand your weaknesses. It's much harder for a person to correct a natural weakness than to improve a strength that comes naturally. Realize that your lowest color is most likely your greatest weakness. My lowest scoring color is Gold, a true indication that organization is my greatest weakness. Someone with a lowest score of Orange most likely is risk averse and not competitive. A lowest score of Blue might not empathize very well. A low score of Green might not be at all analytical or grasp technical points.

It's not easy for someone else to *teach* you about you. But the tools and approach of the color spectrum can *help you learn* more about you. Take this opportunity – it will pay off.

From time to time you may find it useful to go back and re-read the descriptions of each of the personality colors. As you become more familiar with the concepts of the colors, you will find that you gain more insights each time you refresh your knowledge. I know: if you're an Orange you'll find it

57

hard to do this! But the more you understand about the different colors, the more accurately you will be able to apply the approach in your everyday life.

Me and My Color

As the author, my personality is embedded in this book. Understanding my personality type will help you understand what I have to say. Like you, I first had to discover my personality type to change my perceptions of others and my reactions to their behavior. So what sequence am I?

When I created the survey based on the research, I discovered that my primary color is Orange. My other colors, in order are: Blue, Green and Gold.

I am in good company. Lots of salespeople are predominantly Orange. As a strong Orange personality (with a good measure of Blue) it is easy and natural for me to sit down with a customer and immediately begin small talk about sports, their family, current events, and so on. I can build sound relationships quickly – I am naturally outgoing and friendly. I am also highly competitive. Seems ideal for a sales person doesn't it? And in many cases it is, but people like me can become better sales people when we know how to modify our approach to make people at the opposite end of the spectrum – in my case Golds – just as comfortable as my Orange and Blue customers.

.

11. THE RIGHT PERSON IN THE RIGHT JOB

A good way for you to become more familiar with different personality styles is to observe people in their working context, and understand what personality characteristics attract people to one job rather than other, what makes people happy at work rather than disgruntled, and how people gravitate to certain professions.

Don't Put an Orange Peg in a Green Hole

Any of the four personality types can enter any field and be great at what they do. But different personality types are naturally better equipped to excel in different types of job. Are you in a position today that is motivating you to do your best? What is it about your job that motivates you each and every day?

Some people go through life not enjoying a career because they were directed toward that career choice based on their exposed talents, rather than their personality needs. If a student excelled in a specific academic subject, it was assumed that he or she should go into a profession related to that subject. Not always a good idea.

I was one of those people who initially ended up in the wrong job. I received my bachelor's degree in Mechanical Engineering from Rensselaer Polytechnic Institute in Troy, New York and worked as an engineer for seven years before figuring out that as an engineer I was miserable. I finally moved into sales in 1983 and it changed my whole attitude about work. I finally enjoyed what I was doing.

In high school I was near the top of my class in math scores. The school guidance counselor recommended I go into the field of engineering since I was strong in math and science. Being a naive seventeen-year-old, I thought, 'Why not?' I was on the math team in high school and did fairly well, and I thought that going to a prestigious university would be great. Yet in my first year of college I asked myself, 'Why am I taking engineering?' I didn't really understand what it was all about and I had no clue as to why I needed to be an expert with integrals and derivatives. What would I do with them? What are they used for? But I kept going; I was not going to give up on this degree. Understanding now that I am an Orange personality gives me new perspective on why I excelled on the math team and completed my engineering degree, even when I was unhappy with it. Oranges don't quit and hate to lose!

Oranges value competition, love to get attention, are bottom line driven, and concrete thinkers. I was naturally good with numbers, but my drive to excel in math was from a competitive nature to be the best, and not because I was fascinated by the elegance of logarithmic scales — as a Green might be. I wanted to be known in high school as the best in math and wanted all to know I was going to one of the best engineering schools in the country. Yet when I got to college I nearly flunked out. Not exactly what you would expect from my performance in high school.

In retrospect, the reason for the melt-down is easy to see. My goal was *to get into a good school* and once I achieved that goal, *the competition was over*. All I wanted from college was the degree, and there was no obvious reason to compete. Competition is what I value and that is what motivates me. No competition, no motivation - which equated to poor performance. I made it through my four years and received my degree but as I look back it was clear I should have been doing something more suited to my real temperament — such as tackling business school.

When I was in an engineering job, I sat at a desk for eight hours a day and analyzed blueprints: not exactly the type of work that stimulates an Orange personality! Oranges prefer action jobs that keep them moving around and have fun juggling different balls. Excitement and challenges motivate the Orange personality. I simply wasn't cut out to study blueprints all day. It took me seven years to figure that out – but then I moved into computer sales with Digital Equipment Corporation. There I had a great experience for sixteen years in sales, sales management and sales training – all of which played to the strengths of my personality style. I finally was in a career role that made good use of my temperament, working with people every day either training sales people or visiting customers.

If we can understand someone's personality, we have a much better chance of understanding what they value and what will drive a person to deliver their best performance. This means understanding their full personality color spectrum and then putting this knowledge to use.

My primary color is Orange, and my secondary color is Blue. If my early boss had recognized this and understood the motivations and strengths of the various personality colors, he would not have sat me at a desk with the blueprints. He might have sent me into the field or into procurement where my competitive drives and respect for people's feelings would have aided the company. Or he might have tasked me with training the new recruits. If he was really insightful, he would have moved me to a sales job.

Fitting in, in the workplace

Why do some people fit in just fine in a company and others struggle to maintain their position? How is it that an individual can be mediocre in one company, but can become a star when she moves to a different company, even when doing the same type of work?

Part of the answer is that not only do employees have personality, but so do companies. Companies have values, and when they become instilled in the way the company operates, they become part of the company culture. Company culture directs individual behaviors by peer examples and by directly, or indirectly, rewarding specific behaviors. This collective behavior can be said to be a 'company personality'.

Of course, we cannot administer this assessment to corporations. Nevertheless, we can look at corporate values and behaviors and compare them to the characteristics of each personality style. And frequently we react to corporations as if they were individuals and expect actions and judge behaviors as if they were a person. Let me give you some examples, based on my experience, of companies with color-like personalities.

The companies I've worked for in the past had personalities that have either supported my own values as an Orange or made it difficult for me to perform. Their values were different than my own. Most companies have 'mission statements' and 'value statements' that state their intentions as to how they support their employees, customers and the community. Some companies have an entrepreneurial spirit and take more risk than others. Some companies are very controlling while others expect individuals at all levels to act independently to make things happen for the customer. Other companies are very process-oriented and structured: rules and procedure must be followed. There are companies that are technology-driven and perceive technology as their competitive edge. Yet other companies will put their employees first and value them as the company's most important asset. There also are companies that view employees as merely an expense.

If you are an Orange personality who struggles under the control of rules and process, you might be highly frustrated working for a company that has a Gold-ish personality. If you are a Green personality working for a company that is not technology-driven and doesn't put creativity and research as a priority in values, you are likely to experience disappointment.

62

A company that exhibits Blue characteristics by valuing their employees and customers is Southwest Airlines. The company, built by Herb Kelleher, is built around their people and their trust in each other. Southwest seemingly empathizes with each and every traveler. They thrive on fun and making each flight an enjoyable experience. If you are a Blue personality, you would love working for Southwest. If you are Gold, their environment might be too casual and free wheeling for you, especially wearing their non-traditional uniforms. Southwest Airlines is in the customer service business and just happens to make their revenue by flying planes.

If you're a Gold personality you might fit in very well with a nationwide bank or a company like EDS or Perot Systems. They are traditional, formal in nature and have well-defined processes for running their company.

If you are a Green personality, the research labs at Merck, Apple or Hewlett Packard might be a great fit. Creativity, research and development, and engineering are Green core competencies. Working for Digital as an Orange, I had a blast. Even though the founder Ken Olsen did not believe in a commissioned sales force, we had freedom to create and adapt to our customers' needs. Greens and Oranges work well in an environment that gives freedom to create and not restrict.

Nike is an example of an Orange company. The name Nike comes from the Greek goddess of victory. Competition and winning are characteristics of the Orange company personality. Nike's 'Walk of Fame' at their headquarters has Joan Benoit, the winner of the Boston Marathon, John McEnroe the tennis great and Michael Jordan one of the best basketball players ever. With Nike it's about winning. With Nike selling golf shoes, I'm sure Tiger Woods will join this 'Walk of Fame' some day. Just my opinion!

This is not to say that only Green personality styles will be happy working in a Green company, or Orange in an Orange company. There are many roles in every corporation and in the following chapters you will learn, as management, how to best position each personality color. As employees, you will learn how to respond with understanding, and not just blind gut instincts, to the aggregate personality of a company. As a company, you can tailor you messages to each personality – not just your own dominant one. It is all about understanding, and adjusting with perspective to the needs of each personality color. The strength of a great team is understanding and leveraging the strengths of all four personality styles to achieve versatility.

12. MORE ABOUT EACH COLOR

Left Brain, Right Brain

This following illustrates how the brain is segmented by the characteristics of each of the personality style colors.

Green

Rational

Analytical

Critical

Numerical

Realist

Orange

Imagination

Impulsivity

Synthesis

Speculation

Perception

Gold

Organization

Timeliness

Reliability

Judgment

Protection

Blue

Sensitivity

Emotions

Creativity

Feelings

Supportive

The four quadrants of the brain

Learning how the brain is organized helps us understand the unique behaviors and views of each personality style. Left-brain people (Green and Gold) view information and situations differently than right-brain people (Orange and Blue). Greens, using the left front of the brain, focus on being rational and analytical. Golds, using the left back, focus on judgment and organization. The Right-brain personalities, being more subjective, rely more on feelings. For Oranges, using the right front of the brain, focus on imagination and perception. For the Blue, using the right rear quadrant, it's feelings and emotions that dominate their personality.

The left brain is verbal and hears *what is said* while the right brain pays more attention to the non-verbal, which is *how it's said*. The left brain is more serial in looking at events while the right brain sees all at once. The left brain understands the text while the right brain understands the context. Left is about analysis and right is about synthesis. Left-brain people are more into detail and good at solving complicated problems with data, while the right brain is more perceptive and 'big picture' oriented. The left brain is the logical side and the right brain is the creative side. Remember, we all have both sides of the brain and a mix of all four brain quadrants.

As is common knowledge now, science has determined that men's brains and women's brains are wired somewhat differently. This is also reflected in personality colors. More women tend to fall into the Blue category than their male counterparts and a higher percentage of men than women fall into the Green personality group. Women's brains are wired more for empathy and relationships, while men are wired more towards being task-oriented. As an example, women shop and men buy. For women it's an experience, for men it's a task.

Does Personality Change?

A question that regularly occurs in our workshops is 'does your personality change during your life time?' The answer to this is generally 'no' or at least 'not much'. The relative order of colors in our personality spectrum stays the same through our entire life. What might change are the habits and views gained during the events we experience in our life. It can begin at home with our parents, immersed in the environment where we grew up. Did you grow up in a strict home or one that had few rules? Or did your parents give you lots of space to make your own mistakes?

Events that change our view and values can include getting married, having children, and getting a divorce. Our spiritual education also can modify our behavior and approach to life; but at the same time our fundamental personality style can color our spiritual views of life.

What we do for our career will also temper habits we have, for example our reaction to timeliness and organization skills. Let me again use myself as an example. Even though I'm an Orange personality, and Oranges are typically not punctual, but I am never late for meetings. As I am in sales and sales training it would be ludicrous for me to show up late to my own training event. Over the years I have disciplined myself to be early; I have brought forward Gold characteristics, from deeper in my personality spectrum, because this supports my primary driver to win at what I set out to do. Also, growing up with a dad that is never late, certainly had a huge influence!

Another example might be a Green whose natural preference would be to work alone. However, if that person is, say, a technology trainer and is therefore obliged to work closely with people, he or she could pull attitudes from her less prominent Blue-ish personality, and as a result become generally more outgoing.

Blues thrive on sound relationships with people and do not seek conflict. But if a Blue becomes a trial lawyer, that experience will draw out his Orange-ish characteristics. This will modify his attitude towards conflict and confrontation, and therefore his behavior.

A Gold who is very schedule-oriented and traditional might learn different behaviors when placed in a context that requires fast decisions – for example as a physician in an emergency room where rules might sometimes have to be broken to save lives.

Color and Culture

What about personality styles in different cultures? Tests have shown that the percentages of each personality style work out the same throughout the world. Every culture has every personality style in much the same proportions as do ours. However, other cultures, ours included, do develop stereotypes about foreign cultures. Stereotypes come from our perceptions – not from an objective test. So if a person holds a strongly stereotypical view of another culture, which probably tells you more about that person than about that other culture. Different cultures might have strong characteristics like being punctual, being expressive or even being relaxed versus formal.

Still, some cultures place great value on specific characteristics – which correspond with the characteristics of a personality color. Humor can derive from this, where circumstances force a culture to act differently than its perceived primary color, or where acting like the perceived color is inappropriate to the circumstance. In the case of culture, labeling by color is done to cast light on our perceptions, and their internal cultural values, and how we should adjust to these. So it is best done with caution and respect.

From our 'American' view, Brits, Asians and Germans seem more Gold and Green, while Hispanic, Latino and African-American people might appear more Blue and Orange. That is only a perspective from our culture. Germans and Swiss, judging by the importance of train schedules, live by the clock, as Golds do – as a culture, they seemingly value and reward Gold characteristics. People from Mexico are seen

68

as more relationship-oriented, so can be perceived more like a Blue. The English live by the calendar, so be punctual but never too early. The French love to argue and converse and are labeled logical thinkers (after Descartes). But they are also seen as impassioned romantics (after their film style).

These stereotypes may be strongly held, but the reality is that the relative percentages of Blues, Greens, Golds and Oranges is pretty much the same in Mexico as in Germany, England as in France and Japan as in the USA.

Again, we view people through the influences of our own environment. If you visit Tuscany in Italy and you're from Texas, you might think Italy is the most beautiful place on the planet. If you're from Tuscany and visit Napa Valley, you might think that Napa is the most beautiful place you have ever seen. If you're from New York, like me, you've just got to love the spectacular West Texas scenery. (Just kidding!)

Our perspectives on what we value most, what we feel about our homes and how we view other cultures are all very much influenced by our own cultures, but are still consistent with our underlying personality types. Just as our perspectives about our environment and our circumstances in life color our views, so our personality color styles reflect our perspectives of place and culture. Different personalities have different perspectives. We are lucky to have these different perceptions drawn from a full spectrum of personality styles.

Are we different at work and play?

Another question often asked in our workshops is: 'Does my personality style change when in personal situations versus business situations.' The answer is generally 'no'. We are always the same personality style.

However, the way we behave is influenced by the context. We might view relationships with people at work differently than relationships with family and friends. We might have a different attitude to risk at work than in our personal life. The way we buy something for personal use might be a different than the way we make a business purchase, perhaps exposing more personal tastes rather than emphasizing responsibility and accountability.

But overall we find that our primary personality displays certain characteristics that remain consistent in both personal life and in business activity. As an Orange, I am competitive by nature. I value competition in my personal life as I do in my business. Blues value relationships just as much in personal life and in business. Golds always value structure. Greens value knowledge and information in personal and business situations.

But while the underlying preference stays the same, the way we express these preferences in our workplace behavior and social behavior can be quite different.

13. OTHER PEOPLE'S COLORS

Now that you have taken the *Connecting 4 People Assessment* and know your personality color sequence, how can you use this knowledge to establish better communication and stronger relationships?

In order to gain a real appreciation of the variety of attitudes and behaviors encompassed by the personality sequence, you can now appreciate the differences of the people you know well – work colleagues, friends and family. Most people enjoy doing assessments like this, and find the results interesting. The ten-question assessment has been designed to be straightforward to apply and interpret and you will soon learn how it works.

After a few assessments, you'll start to identify patterns in the results, and will become familiar with the behaviors that signify certain personality groupings. And you will increasingly be able to understand, and empathize with, the different attitudes to *values* that underpin these different behaviors. What we value most establishes our motives for what we desire and how we behave.

Flip this around: *not* knowing someone else's personality color means we might not know what they value, and therefore we will judge their behavior from our color perspective, not from theirs. These kind of misperceptions in our interactions with them can in turn alter their perceptions of us. Daniel Goleman says in *Social Intelligence*, 'As we alter our perceptions, we can change our emotions.' For many people their perception is their only reality – in that they may not be questioning their viewpoint! You can now learn how to avoid this error and make it easier to identify with your customers.

Back in Chapter 3, I described an incident from early in my career when I became defensive because I misinterpreted the customer's attitude. I thought I was being challenged when he was actually seeking information. This customer was a Green personality type. Knowing what I do today, if I had established upfront that he was a 'Green', I would have approached the sales call with a clearer understanding of (a) what motivated the client and (b) how my own personality style affected my understanding of his behavior. Greens are inquisitive by nature and always ask tough questions. My client was reflecting his desire for information and detail, not questioning my knowledge. As an Orange, I saw competition and he, as a Green, wanted an information resource.

Today, knowing that I am dealing with a Green client totally changes my perspective of the person and my behavior and approach. Knowing someone's personality will change your view of the situation too.

Greens are often uncomfortable with small talk, will ask lots of questions, are slower to make decisions, look for all the possible alternatives, and consider the future – exploring what opportunities might result from your solution. Now, whenever I identify a Green, I expect all that and I respond accordingly.

I'd like to share some more experiences that helped me develop my own interest in personality styles.

My brother Scott called me on the phone and announced 'I've got Dad on the phone.' Since Dad and Scott do not live in the same city, I jumped to the conclusion that if they were together on this call, there must be some type of emergency going on. Immediately my heart rate was peaking and I was ready to hop on a plane. I asked 'Is everything all right?' Then Scott reassured me: 'Stu, everything is fine. I just loaded this new phone conference software program and thought I'd test it by conferencing us all together.' As an Orange, my first reaction was to leap to the challenge – but there was no challenge. Instead, we had a pleasant conversation, the three of us talking about the kids, our golf game, and generally joking around.

Everything was going along nicely, but after five minutes Dad abruptly said 'It's time to go' and he hung up! Had we said something to upset him?

Now if you didn't know our Dad's personality you might think he was mad at us, but we know him well, and realized he wasn't. Our Dad's primary personality color is Gold. Golds live a highly scheduled life. Knowing that, my brother suggested that according to his daily routine, it was the time for Dad to collect the mail!

Golds are like that. Several months earlier my wife Betty and I visited my Dad in Florida. We expected a prompt pickup from Dad but were left waiting at baggage claim. Why? It turned out that the reason we had to wait a little longer was because he had to attend a scheduled dental appointment. Our flights were booked two months in advance and you would think it would be easy to reschedule the dental appointment to pick us up on time, but that's not how Dad's personality is wired. Instead of getting annoyed at this, we understand that with a Gold, just don't expect a schedule to be changed.

Our brother Jay was a Gold. From the age of twelve, each Saturday morning he would wake up at 8am and put together his schedule for the day. Golds are extremely organized. You can see this in their bedroom closet where all the shirts are in order by color; shoes are perfectly in a row; pants and suits segregated by season. I have one Gold friend that actually alphabetizes his soups in the pantry.

Ask a Gold what it means when they see a speed limit sign of 70 mph and they will say it's the law and you should go 70. Ask an Orange what it means to them and they will say it's merely a suggestion. A Green will automatically add in an overage allowance and then drive at 77 expecting no risk of a ticket. To a Blue it means stay close to 70, because otherwise you'll upset someone and get in trouble.

Trying to view situations from other people's perspective is the first step in understanding why each personality behaves differently. We start to understand their priorities and motivations. We build an appreciation of *why* people do things, not just what they do.

Use with Care and Consideration

There are some rules we need to understand when we start using our approach with colors. Here are five of the most important:

1- Don't stereotype people

2- Don't try to change people

3- Don't negate the values of others

4- Don't let strengths become liabilities

5- Do validate the strengths of each color

Don't stereotype people based on their dominant personality style. Not all Blues are the same; and this is true for the other three colors too. Everyone is unique in ways that even their full personality sequence cannot completely capture and classify. However, the dominant personality style will have certain characteristics that all have in common.

Let's look at an example of this. My primary color is Orange and my secondary is Blue. My wife Betty is also Orange but her second color is Gold. Even though we have a lot of the same characteristics, sharing Orange as our dominant color, we also have differences. As indicated by my second color testing Blue, I am more right-brained than my wife and generally more sensitive to others feelings. I don't handle conflict as well as Betty. With Gold as her second color, Betty is more structured: she has worked at AT&T for thirty-three years. We find that Golds value loyalty and so also give their loyalty, which is fortunate for me. Betty's lowest ranked color is Blue; her favorite saying at work is 'cry a river, build a bridge, and get over it'. Not exactly something a Blue personality would like to hear!

The danger of stereotyping is that by assuming that someone conforms exactly to the textbook description of their dominant color, you can miss important aspects of their true personality.

Don't try to change people. The full power of the color spectrum approach appears when you use the strengths of people as you find them, and find ways to work around their weaknesses.

Don't negate the value of others. People naturally give more weight to their own strengths and when they see these strengths displayed by others they understand their importance, since those capabilities are directly related to what they themselves value and what motivates them to perform. However, this means that sometimes people can undervalue or negate the value that other personalities bring. Just because it's something we aren't good at or don't enjoy doesn't mean that it doesn't have value.

We should never negate the value that other personalities bring to a team or a project. There is much strength in diversity.

Don't let strengths become a liability. We tend to overdo it with things we are naturally good at. Even though Golds are good at organization and structure, we don't want to over emphasize this to the point that we miss out on creative ideas that produce positive change. Greens are always able to come up with new ideas. But there comes a point when the new ideas have to stop and implementation starts, not always a Green strength.

Do validate the strengths of each color. When you've assessed the dominant color of someone, it's tempting to assume that they fit the specification of that color. However sometimes people don't exactly fit the pattern, because we're all different and the color spectrum approach is, after all just a useful model, not reality itself. Therefore, before you make a decision on the basis of an assumed strength (or preference, or attitude) test it out first. You should always confirm your supposition before you put it into action.

14. Building a Sales Team

A good way of becoming familiar with the power of the personality assessment is to use it in your own work environment. You can build your understanding of the method and grow to become friends with all the colors, by using your knowledge of the personality spectrum in your sales team. Whether you are a member of a sales team, or a sales manager, you can start the ball rolling by introducing your colleagues to the program, encouraging them to take the survey, and by using the profiles in your everyday life.

If applied correctly, you and your team will certainly find the approach helpful. In addition, you will be learning more about the spectrum in a relatively friendly environment. This will prepare you well for applying the principles of personality styles in your interactions with customers.

People from each of the four basic personality styles enter the profession of sales. In our sales training workshops, we administer the Connecting 4 People Assessment and then sort the students into groups by primary color. When we ask our groups in the workshop which personality is best in sales, everyone shouts out their primary color. In fact, each of the four colors can be effective in sales – but for entirely different reasons. It is not about *what* they do (they all sell for a living) it's about *why*.

What drives each color to sell? For the Blue it's about meeting clients and building strong, long lasting relationships. For the Gold, it's about the systematic, ordered process of selling. They take pride in their company, typically leading with the strengths of the company. The Green salesperson wants to solve the client's problems, and enjoys coming up with the best possible solutions. For the Orange it's about winning: beat the competition, build a lasting relationship with the client and keep on winning!

Sales people don't have to deal just with customers. They interact with others in their own company as a member of or leader of one or more teams: an account team, a project team, or regional management team. No one succeeds alone. We all need admin support, technical support and someone else to bounce ideas off. Effective teams are basic to business success, including the success of sales teams and sales individuals.

If you want to build a winning sales team, everyone should understand about personality styles and receive training in the Connecting 4 People approach. At the very least they should all read this book!

Leadership Personality Styles

We all know people who can be described as great leaders. But are they great leaders all the time?

I'm a big football fan, and so I keep a close eye on the performance of my favorite team, the Dallas Cowboys. In 2004, Cowboys fans were disappointed with the mediocre performance of a once-great team, so we were excited when the famous coach Bill Parcells agreed to come out of retirement to coach the Cowboys. Bill had a great record of taking on losing teams and turning them into champions. He had turned the New York Giants, New York Jets and the New England Patriots. Clearly a great coach, and everyone expected him to do it again with the Cowboys.

At first it looked promising, as the Cowboys made the playoffs. However, after that it was all downhill, for three disappointing years. In 2006, Parcells resigned his position as coach, and Jerry Jones, the team owner announced that Wade Phillips would take his place.

Wade's history was with the San Diego Chargers and the Buffalo Bills. Fans weren't sure what to expect. But when the 2007 season started you immediately saw the difference on the sidelines. Tony Romo's second season as the Cowboy's quarterback was one to remember. What was only recently a fragmented team had started to pull together, no longer putting their individual interests before the interests of the team. Under Wade Phillips, thirteen starts later, the Cowboys were heading to the playoffs after a 12-1 season.

Wade Phillips succeeded where Bill Parcells had fallen short, apparently. Yet Parcells had a wonderful past record, and Phillips, while no slouch, did not appear to have that golden touch – until he took on the Cowboys.

What happened? I don't know for sure, but here's my hunch. It was all about matching personality to the team. Parcells' personality as a leader worked for some teams but not for the Cowboys. Phillips' personality worked brilliantly for the Cowboys, who became enthused, energetic and cooperated with each other, all aspects of their performance that had been lacking under Parcells.

Any personality type can be a leader, but different personalities lead in different ways. We need to understand each color's leadership style so the different team members know what to expect; and so team leaders themselves can understand the impact their personality can have on the team members and on team performance.

Let's use a simple example to illustrate some differences in the way different personality types go about building and leading a team. The 'leader' has just purchased a gas barbeque grill: how would each personality lead a team of their friends in assembling the grill?

The **Blue** personality would make it a fun event. A Blue would invite friends over to help out, and would make sure that everyone was engaged and getting along. Afterwards the group would socialize together around the grill to celebrate the successful assembly of the barbeque. If the grill was still in pieces in the yard and people were getting tired and hungry, the Blue would happily order pizza and leave the barbeque for another time.

A **Gold** would schedule exactly three hours for the task. After determining how many helpers were needed, the Gold would call some friends. Golds are good at enlisting help. The Gold would have the team study the list of parts and systematically organize the parts to match the illustration. Then they would read the assembly instructions step by step. Each friend would have a role and be assigned specific tasks in sequence.

A **Green** would call some friends and discuss grill functions. Those that seemed to know 'what was what' would be invited over to help assemble it. Together they would open the box, pull everything out and look at the picture of the assembled grill. The instructions would be checked when tricky parts occurred. There would be a lot of discussion about how the instructions could be better written and the product design improved. In the end they would fire up the grill to test it – grilling everything at hand to get a large test sample. In their discussion of the grill's performance they would agree to order some cool optional extras – an attached grill light and a rotisserie.

The **Orange** would really have preferred to buy the grill already assembled. Unable to find one at a good price, the Orange would invite over some friends, definitely including some Greens, to help assemble it as fast as possible. To make sure they come, the Orange would bribe them with a big spread of food and drink – to celebrate the purchase. There's a good chance the party will start before the grill gets done!

The Blue Leader

Blue personalities are rarely in a leadership position, preferring to facilitate. While they make excellent leaders because of their compassion for people, they care less for organizational skills and structure. Success of their people is more important than the goal of the team.

Leadership abilities: Blues are good at reading people and understanding the strengths that the individuals will bring to the team. They are good at motivating others with their casual and communicative nature.

Leadership style: Blues are open-minded and accommodating. They will lead by consensus and are always available for their people. They tend to be liked by all their subordinates. Blues are not into power and control, giving freedom to their workers. They are optimistic and encourage creativity and cooperation within the team.

Leadership shortcomings: Blues don't like making tough and unpopular decisions. Blues have a tough time giving bad news to people. They will avoid conflict. This can lead to missed deadlines, or results falling short.

The Gold Leader

Golds are a natural for a leadership role. Golds are dedicated to the company and the company comes first.

Leadership abilities: Golds are very good at process and procedure. They are consistent, predictable and very stable when in the role of the leader. They will not ask the unreasonable of their workers.

Leadership style: Golds expect everyone to follow process and procedure. Golds are goal-oriented and expect everyone to do their share. Golds set clear expectations with the team members. They require their teams to complete all tasks and insist on follow up. Golds follow set schedules and agendas to manage everyone's activity. Meetings are orderly; they always include a reason for the meeting, an agenda, and a goal.

Leadership shortcomings: Golds want constant updates on individual progress toward completing tasks, assignments or projects. Golds do not put freethinking as a high priority.

The Green leader

Greens are often visionary leaders. Bill Gates and Steve Jobs are good examples. Greens focus on the future and the possibilities in the future. Greens value expertise above other qualities in team members.

Leadership abilities: People will gladly follow a strong vision when it's well thought out. Greens love innovation. Greens like to streamline process in order to be more efficient. They are constantly looking to make things better.

Leadership style: Green leaders value competence and great ideas. They will be skeptical in their approach. Don't expect a lot of small talk from a Green leader. They will ask a lot of questions, taking longer to make a decision as they weigh all the information presented to them.

Leadership shortcomings: Greens are not as motivating as a Blue or Orange personality. They also tend to rearrange information multiple times, which causes frustration for some team members.

The Orange leader

Orange leaders are the energizers. Orange leaders encourage, inspire, and have great endurance. They make the most optimistic, positive leaders.

Leadership abilities: It's natural for Oranges to spur on the team and set a fast pace. If a crisis occurs the Orange leader will jump right in to help fix it.

Leadership style: The Orange leader won't sit around, so you typically won't find them behind a desk. They like to be in the trenches, engaged with a client, a partner, or a vendor. They are buddies with the troops and thrive on being around team members.

Leadership shortcomings: Paperwork, process, agendas and a lot of meetings are bothersome for the action-oriented Orange leader. They will delegate what they consider non-exciting, boring tasks. Hearing murmuring and complaining is not good for Orange ears.

Building a Team

Building a winning team takes more than talent. The team leader must have the right attitude, whatever his or her personality style. And the team leader must bring together people who can work productively together to achieve the goals of the team, and of the company.

I am proud of my brother, Scott. He has been with Avon for a number of years and it seems wherever Avon sends him, the sales numbers rise. Scott was President of Avon for 15 of their subsidiaries on four continents around the world.

Scott connects with the people in his organization. As a Blue, Scott does this naturally, but he takes it further than most. He understands the need to build a winning culture. Jason Young, in his book *Culturetopia* says: 'A Culturetopian company always makes best use of people's strengths and finds ways to work around their weaknesses'. This is exactly what Scott does well, and it pays off. Scott knows that, with the right leadership, differences can make a team stronger. And he also knows that doing what you're good at, having fun, and delivering great performance are all linked.

Understanding personality styles can make a huge difference when it comes to team interaction and team performance. In successful teams the leader creates an environment in which team members interact smoothly and take on responsibility and accountability, and everyone is energized and motivated to achieve the team's goals. Understanding the personality styles of the team members helps the leader create that environment.

Knowing their own personality style, and those of their colleagues, allows each team member to adjust their behavior and accommodate the communications styles and needs of the other personality types.

Lastly, finding and agreeing to a composite personality style for the group allows all the members to fit into a clear group style: a 'how,' to complement the tasks of the group, their 'what'.

Our personality-based approach should work for any team: sales team, customer service team an information technology consulting team, or a football team. All kinds of teams can have their performance enhanced by understanding what strengths the members bring to the team.

It is also important to know what weaknesses exist and how to accommodate for these. Just imagine a team of all Blues, Golds, Greens or Oranges and what those teams would be lacking! There would be no balance if everyone was the same. It would be difficult to harness skills and knowledge and turn this into results. They might not be able to handle conflict, or might be too structured, or lack creativity, or have no organization skills. Imagine a team if everyone wanted to work alone or if no one was allowed time alone to think and create. Imagine a team of all Oranges who want to delegate the details, but no one would accept what is being assigned to them!

Organize teams with people in positions suitable to their personality strengths, and compensating for their weaknesses. This will maximize the team's performance - resulting in both efficiency and effectiveness.

Personality and teamwork

Understanding the personality styles of your team members will bring teamwork and leadership to a new level. We begin to understand and accept why each individual behaves differently. We understand the unique characteristics of what motivates each personality, how they make decisions, how they view risk and conflict, and how they like to communicate. It adds a dimension of understanding that did not exist before. What once seemed like random inappropriate behavior, now is understood as the interaction of different personality styles. It helps to understand why one individual behaves one way and another responds to a situation differently.

After understanding the differences, we must accept them. Only then, can we make appropriate use of these different characteristics. Understanding which individuals have certain strengths helps us to know who will respond best in specific situations. In the end, it comes down to maximizing team performance by leveraging the unique talents of the team members.

Ivan Boyd was Chief Revenue Officer at GTESS Corporation based in Richardson, Texas. Over the last two years his team has gone through our personality styles workshop. When the team has a quarterly meeting the conversation always includes comments along the lines of: 'Of course Jim will get that done, he's an Orange'; or 'Rick should take a look at that because he's Green'. As a team, last year Jim and Rick closed the two largest deals in the history of the company by understanding their styles as well as the personality styles of the buying decision makers.

- They tailored their team approach to the specifics needed to motivate the specific personality style of the client. So knowing their customer contact was say, a Green, they could reset their strategy to match.

- They switched roles, to lead or follow, based on whether the client would respond better to a Green or an Orange personality. This included building specific relationships with different members of the buying team, based on pairing each with their complementary personality match.

- Lastly, they reinforced each other as a team. For example, Jim, the Orange, need not fear deep questions, because Rick, the Green, was there to answer them.

At GTESS Corporation, account reviews of all customer contacts now are categorized by their personality style. The corporation's service organization and IT group know their personality styles; GTESS maximized team performance across all the company disciplines.

When we know an individual's personality style, we understand much more about they way they will respond to different people, their approach to problems, and we see how it might differ from ours. The results and improvements in team performance can be extra-ordinary.

Now let's look at the characteristics of each of the personalities in a team setting.

The Blue team member

Blues are interested in the well-being of the team. They promote cooperation and collaboration. They will be the first to welcome a new member to the team. For them, it's all about people and relationships. Blues are caring and honest with everyone on the team. They focus on the strengths of each team member.

Blues need to know that they are doing a good job. Giving them positive feedback is important to keep them motivated. They will build up and promote other team members. Blues encourage co-workers in their positions. They avoid confrontation and conflict, and can be slow to make decisions.

Blues will consider all the people involved when making a decision, examining each possibility, taking time for their decisions. In a situation where there is potential change, a Blue will be cautious. They are not big risk takers.

The Gold team member

Gold personalities are strong at organization. They are usually the workhorse on the team and live by the clock. When work needs to be completed, a Gold is just the person to accomplish it – on time and on budget. They are good at watching the details and getting things right. Golds are reliable.

A Gold feels most at home in a structured environment. Golds do not want their time wasted. They want to know what to expect and expect an agenda with every meeting. Scheduling is important and so is timeliness. Sometimes Golds over-stress the importance of structure, at the expense of flexibility and creativity.

Gold personalities like to be in control. Golds are extremely dedicated to the cause of the company. Golds measure their worth to an organization by the work they get done. They expect everyone to work just as hard as they do. They can become frustrated if they are told to rush to completion what was not planned properly at the start. Golds do not like change and will question why change needs to occur.

The Green team member

Greens are the best at solving problems. For the Green, work is play and they can go for hours on end till they solve a problem. Expect more questions from a Green than the other personalities. The Green personality wants to first understand the big picture before they dig deep into research and analysis. They will look at all the possibilities. They like challenges in work and look for creative solutions.

Greens are more independent and enjoy working alone and without distractions. Information is more intriguing to a Green than the relationships with people on the team. Understanding team members' emotions is not of great importance to a Green. They will miss the clues that relationships are in trouble until a situation blows up in their faces; then they treat the event like a problem to be solved. Small talk can be a distraction to a Green.

Competency and knowledge are of most value to Greens. Freedom is important to a Green: allow them to be creative and come up with new ideas. Expect debate and challenge on issues since this is part of their nature. Sometimes bringing a project to completion is a weakness for a Green; often they will leave the details of the execution of what they created to others to complete. Greens can overdo debate and might over analyze data, thereby slowing down decisions.

The Orange team member

Oranges are the cheerleaders of the team; they like to spur the others on to finish the task. Their mantra is like Nike, 'Just do it!' Orange's philosophy is to work hard and play hard. They are competitive; everything is about winning and looking good. Oranges thrive on risks and challenges. They prefer tangible problems since they are concrete thinkers and are bottom line driven. Putting out fires is a pleasure for an Orange.

Oranges are usually the best at reading others and adapting a style that would be acceptable to them. Oranges will entertain the team and keep the momentum up.

An Orange worker is often impatient. They prefer to get started on a project or task and not sit around and brainstorm or plan for long periods of time. They need to multi-task since they get bored staying on one task too long. Oranges like their independence. Speed and action are important to an Orange's environment; too many meetings are not a good thing, especially if they go on too long.

Oranges are more tactical than they are strategic: 'Just let us figure things out as we go along and we'll get it done.' Oranges like to delegate and they look at the big picture. They'll leave the details to the others like the Greens and Golds. They are more interested in the results than the process to get there. Planning is not their strength, performance is.

Teams that work

We find that winning teams all have the following characteristics:

Explicit trust between all the team members. The leader is just another team member and everyone is a 'wing man'. Trust is more than honesty; it is knowledge that all their co-workers *will* perform.

Explicit trust of the leader by the team - and also the leader must trust their team.

Open communication between the members and the leader.

An environment that inspires new ideas.

Members hold each other accountable while not being judgmental.

Willing to take risk.

Responsibilities are defined and rewards follow performance.

Members can influence the team with their thoughts and opinions.

Mistakes are viewed as a learning experience.

Each member is valued for their unique gifts and talents – personality style.

Members rely on each other – interdependence.

Everyone knows the team's mission and vision.

Back in the mid '80s, I was on a sales team that worked together and put the team's goals first. Often in sales, team member's work as individuals by themselves. This happens because each salesperson has a personal sales quota for the year. As an experiment, for one year we worked the budget goals for the good of the entire team. The team was as focused on the team goal as their individual goal. That year our team was number one in the US achieving 286% of budget! Teams work best together when everyone has their eye on the same goal: whether it's a sales quota, a customer service quota, or a Super Bowl win. Team members must trust each other and support each other, in order to maximize the strengths of the team. When you have a winning team, you will see momentum that builds as time goes on.

Let's look at another example where extraordinary results happened because each team member valued the personality-driven contributions from the other team members. Years ago a team brainstormed 'how to resolve power lines falling when snow built up on the lines in the northwest.' A Blue noticed the meeting was getting tense. To ease tension, she jokingly expressed a wild idea based on her observations in her garden: 'Birds fly past branches and clip the snow off with their wings – so, could they harness birds?' An Orange laughed, but knowing that anything goes in a brainstorming session, turned to support this notion. At first there were general objections

90

but the Gold facilitator reminded the group: 'There is no judgment on ideas while brainstorming.'

Now, presented with a formal challenge, a Green figured out that if helicopters could fly over the lines, the down-draft would knock off the snow. Having a workable answer, the Gold closed the meeting with assignments for getting it documented and carried out. A team can work most effectively together by having respect for everyone's ideas and contributions.

Problem teams

Let's take a quick look at what characteristics we *don't* want to have in a team. Patrick Lencioni relates these in the book *The Five Dysfunctions of a Team*. The five elements of a poorly performing team are:

1. Absence of trust
2. Fear of conflict
3. Lack of commitment
4. Avoidance of accountability
5. Inattention to results

A team can never perform without trust. Trust allows a team to be honest with each other and their leader. Without trust members will not be able to confront the reality of the problems they encounter.

There will always be problems and when problems occur, so follows conflict. Some people shy away from conflict; however, conflict is healthy. When a team can successfully work through conflict, they know each other better and establish tighter bonds.

Teams typically perform their best when everyone gets on board with the challenge at hand. If there is no commitment, there's no enthusiasm; and without enthusiasm, there is no energy. Teams thrive on the energy that comes from individual members establishing bi-directional relationships that establish and reinforce bonds by meeting each others needs.

Teams must have clear goals and directions. Without goals, there is no accountability. Accountability allows every member to understand what he is or is not contributing, and how he can perform better. The team as a unit must also be accountable to meeting its goals. Even if some members perform, if everyone isn't on board, the team loses.

The last dysfunction is inattention to results. Paired with goals/accountability is the need to take corrective action when shortfalls occur. When the individual team members put their needs before those of the team, neither they nor the team advanced. Rewards and motivation must reinforce cooperative behavior. When team goals take priority over personal goals, the team moves forward.

Why conflict arises in teams

Conflict occurs naturally whenever people work together or live together. We know that everyone is different, yet it is still our natural tendency to view situations from our perspective and not that of the others. When conflict arises, it helps to understand others' personality styles in order to minimize the amount and magnitude of disruptive emotional behavior. If we understand each other's styles, we can be more successful at improving our work environment.

Many teams shy away from conflict, but conflict exposes the possibilities that a team needs to explore. Conflict is a natural outcome of communication with two or more people. Conflict comes from team members having different priorities, values, and views. If we understand each of the four personality styles we can better understand why conflict occurs which can bring issues and problem events to a quicker resolution.

92

Let's explore personalities in conflict on an imaginary customer service team. Our team contains all four personalities led by an Orange. An emergency arises with a customer service problem. Let's visualize the dynamics of the team individuals and their different personalities.

The reaction: The Orange manager calls an immediate meeting of the entire team, to start in fifteen minutes. No pre-established agenda for the meeting exists. Everyone shows up to the meeting with their personal perceptions and needs.

Coming into the meeting: The Gold is upset since she has her routine and has a deadline for an assignment in two hours. The Blue is worried what the customer might think of the team and the company and will our relationship be at risk? The Oranges want it fixed immediately and the Greens want to know the cause.

During the meeting: The Gold wants to know the time schedule for the meeting. The Oranges want to get to the bottom line, go out and fix the problem and get out of the meeting. The Greens have plenty of questions on the root causes of the problem and how to alleviate the problem so it doesn't happen again. The Blues are concerned that the others in the room are getting irritated.

Conflict: The Blues and Greens want to spend the time needed to think everything through. The Oranges and Golds want to end the meeting and solve the problem. Oranges will just figure it out as they go with no details and the Golds want a process.

Why? Blues value the customer relationship and team members concerns; Golds value the process; Greens value finding the cause and the solution; and Oranges value a quick fix.

This meeting is ripe for conflict and argument! However, if everyone could be aware of their own and others' personality styles, they would have a whole new perspective of how each individual would most likely respond to a situation, and better understand their behavior and approach. Team members can respect their differences by understanding what each member values and by leveraging each other's strengths.

Sources of excessive conflict

Some people like conflict now and again. For Greens, assertive debate can help everyone to get to the right answer. For Golds, conflict is an opportunity to wield power and authority. For Blues, it is important for people to bring differences to the surface in order to build sound relationships. Oranges like to compete, and conflict of any sort offers another chance to come out on top.

However excessive conflict can ruin relationships, diminish productivity, and destroy sales opportunities. Sales people and business managers need to be able to understand the point at which healthy discussion is about to move into disruptive conflict, and make sure that things don't reach that point.

Personality plays a very important part in the development of conflict situations. Understanding the way conflict can emerge from the interaction of different personality styles is critical to being able to predict, avoid, and reduce conflict. Whether the conflict arises between a sales person and the customer, or between a team leader and team members, or within a team, those personality sequence features can always provide useful insights.

I'd like to discuss three areas in which conflict can be generated by personality differences:

Different assumptions – where different people have different expectations, motives or priorities, and conflict arises because everyone assumes the other person thinks just like they do.

94

Minor irritations that grow large – where different people respond in different ways to the characteristic behaviors of others.

Stressful circumstances – where people fail to appreciate that others respond to stress and handle it in a variety of ways.

Different personalities, different assumptions

Conflicts often emerge from a mismatch of **expectations**, **motives**, or **priorities**.

If **expectations** are not clearly spelled out then some team members will be surprised, upset or disappointed by what is delivered by others. Each personality type has different key expectations.

Different personality styles have different values; therefore, their **motives** can be different. A challenge that motivates a Gold team member might turn off an Orange – and vice versa – so having them work together on the same task might cause friction.

Priorities for getting work accomplished can also vary among personality types. What is top priority for one team member might be lowest priority for another. For example, an Orange will almost always set a tougher target for a project completion date than a Green. But the Green will always set a higher standard for acceptable quality than an Orange. The Green priority is for best quality while the Orange priority is for quickest completion.

Each color responds differently to pressure, deadlines and control. Each personality style has a different sense of urgency based on what they value. Oranges want to get it out and let it fly; Greens want to hold it close until it is right. Blues and Golds are more resistant to change. Golds and Oranges make decisions faster than Blues and Greens.

95

If we can understand each other's expectations, motives and priorities, we can avoid some conflicting situations. How? By being explicit about what needs to be done and why. By not making assumptions about others' expectations, values and priorities. By not making the mistake of assuming that everyone else is just like you.

Irritating behavior

Conflict can also result from personality characteristics that tend to irritate other people who have different personality styles. All four dominant personality styles have different values, communication styles, and approaches to work, and these differences can cause stress within relationships.

The following color characteristics that can irritate the other personalities leading to tension. Sometimes the irritation reaches a level that moves the tension up a level, into strife.

Blues can be too idealistic, too emotional, go too deep into topics with no closure, be too familiar or agreeable and talk about too many personal issues. To other personality types, sometimes the Blue approach seems wildly off track.

Golds can be too inflexible, too controlling or bossy, too judgmental, call too many meetings and get too bogged down on details. Sometimes their approach seems egotistical, power hungry or stifling to other colors.

Greens can be slow to make decisions, ask too many questions, like to rework things to perfection. They question authority, give too deep an explanation, are too wordy, and too distant. Their approach often seems needlessly complicated to the other colors.

Oranges can be careless about details, impulsive, and impatient. They tend to ignore policy and procedure, they don't report problems, and they're not great at planning

96

ahead. Blues may find Oranges too competitive. Sometimes Greens feel Oranges jump the gun before the time is right.

When someone is behaving in an irritating way, we all have a natural inclination to assume that his or her behavior is purposeful and intentional; you think: 'This is irritating me, so this person is doing it on purpose'. Yes, some personality characteristics can be wearisome and irritating for those with different personality styles. But ask around – other people might be quite happy with what is going on. Maybe it's you. (Or, more likely, maybe you both need to make some adjustments.)

If you understand the impact your natural personality-driven behavior can have on others, it will help you to temper your behavior and thus minimize irritation and stress in others. If you understand that the behavior of some others is so irritating because of personality differences (not just because the other person is being deliberately provocative) then, possibly, those weird behaviors will grow less weird, and less irritating.

Handling stress

Sometimes conflict arises simply from a stressful environment, when everyone is tired. For example, when a hardworking team is tackling a complex project with tight timelines – and then the deadline is brought forward a few days. Or when a big proposal is due, everyone has been working around the clock, and then the customer changes the requirements specification, but not the due date.

Some people will respond to a crisis by behaving unreasonably towards others, others by withdrawing into solitude. When fatigue sets in, introverts re-energize by being alone whereas extraverts re-energize around people.

Often, under situations of pressure, stress and fatigue the personality characteristics of everyone become more accentuated. In the worst case:

Greens flood the team with information and ideas in an attempt to get everyone to save time by just getting on and doing it the Green way.

Blues lose sight of the business objective and concentrate on the personal needs of themselves and others, even when some others would rather forget their personal needs and get the job done.

Oranges leap into action (any action will do) and expect everyone else to do the same. Plan? No time for that.

Golds become even more authoritative than usual, insist on sticking to the process (even if the process wasn't designed for the situation) and demand sacrifices.

Each personality color will respond differently to issues that arise on the team. Conflict arises when these responses are markedly different or directly opposed to what other team members value.

Practical hints for handling conflict

When you encounter a conflict situation, then you should be aware that people behave most closely to their personality type when stressed. This not only accentuates the disruptive aspects of their behavior, as described above, but provides us with some clues as to how best to handle the conflict.

Resolving conflict with Blues:

Be pleasant,

Empathize with their concerns,

Don't be judgmental,

Focus on the people aspects of the resolution.

Resolving conflict with Golds:

Define the issues,

Don't criticize their position,

Be responsible for your actions,

Be respectful.

Resolving conflict with Greens:

Avoid emotion,

Don't insult their intelligence,

Focus on the facts,

Encourage discussion and debate.

Resolving conflict with Oranges:

Don't take their challenge of you as personal

Be flexible

Be realistic

Offer alternatives

The ability to prevent or resolve conflict is a critical skill learned by every successful business person and by every winning team. Resolving conflict is healthy: done correctly, team and customer relationships can advance to greater productivity, greater resilience, and greater achievement. By understanding what each personality values, we gain a pathway to mitigating conflict, strengthening relationships, and building teams that achieve their goals.

15. A PRACTICAL GUIDE TO COLOR ASSESSMENT IN THE FIELD

In the last chapter I concluded by pointing out that if you understanding someone's personality it will help you understand *why* they are doing what they are doing. But how do you assess their personality type?

Early on in a customer relationship it is hardly ever practical or appropriate to sit a customer down and ask them to take the *Connecting 4 People Assessment*. No matter how enthusiastic you are about the color spectrum don't just walk up to a customer and give them the test!

Later on, when you know a customer well, giving the *Assessment* to your customer's decision team is a great ground-breaker, giving value to you and your customer for very little cost and time. But we have found that that this is best done during a planned meeting after you have already developed a sound relationship with your sponsor.

Without the test, however, it is not always easy to accurately identify someone's personality style. So do we have a Catch-22? You need to have established a good relationship in order to sit a client down for the ten-question test; however, to build that degree of familiarity in the relationship, you need to know their color.

Fortunately, there are some ways in which we can gain clues and insights that allow us to gather sufficient information to make a confident assessment of someone's dominant personality color type, and perhaps even the secondary too. The beauty of the assessment is that it is easier than other systems to obtain a good approximation of someone's personality type through observation and discussion. However, it still requires careful thought and discipline to get it right. For an accurate assessment of an individual, he or she must complete the survey form. Casual assessment in the field without the formal assessment can work really well, but should be used with care and consideration.

How do you narrow it down fast? Blue, Gold, Green or Orange? With experience, this will actually become as natural as remembering someone's name. But for beginners, this is the most difficult task in applying our color personality system. While you cannot beat the actual test for accuracy, you can make a good guess. Here are some tips to help you quickly immediately identify someone's personality style.

What are the odds?

This is a lot like playing poker – homework is important. You need to learn the character of the game before you can use it and you learn the odds to judge your strategy. It turns out that personality color styles are not evenly spread in the population.

Most personality models point to an approximate percentage of the population for each color.

Gold is in the 40% range

Orange is around 33%

Blue about 15%

Green around 12%.

Meeting a random person on the street it is two times more likely that you are talking to an Orange than a Blue. Three out of four people you meet will be either Orange or Gold. One in seven will be Blue. And only one in eight will be Green.

Most of the time, you will be meeting Gold and Orange personalities because they make up most of the population.

102

However, because of their specific likes, colors will gravitate to specific activities. So while meeting a Blue or Green in a random group of five is unlikely, this will increase if you are at meetings or places associated with their interests. So when you find a Green, the probability of finding another Green in that setting goes up dramatically.

The location, environment, or activity where you meet someone will change the odds of finding certain colors. In the executive suite, it's more likely they are Gold. In the development or engineering organization, it is likely they are a Green. Human resources and marketing would lean towards Blue. At a sporting event, Oranges are likely to dominate the crowd.

Ask and listen

When you're interacting with customers try to get into the habit of looking for clues to help you identify their personality style. It is important to consistently keep in the forefront of your mind: 'What personality color am I dealing with right now?' The more you do this, the more accurate you will become in your judgments of their personality.

Try to extend the conversation and listen to what they have to say *and how they say it*. Listen for not only **what** is said (facts and information) but **how** it is said (feelings and attitudes).

Every sales person knows to ask the customer the basic question: 'What do you need?' However, in the quest for personality clues, you must widen the conversation to cover areas such as:

'What is most important to you?'

'What do you see as your greatest challenge and your top priorities?'

'What would your approach be?'

Clearly it is seldom necessary or appropriate to ask these questions right out. The idea is to guide the conversation around these topics in a way that is relevant to the business you are discussing.

There are many more questions that you might ask. Remember to listen to their answers and take guidance from the clues communicated by the customer - when openings occur, probe deeper into their challenges and into their view of 'their' situation. We can more easily influence each sale if we understand our customer's personality and their perspectives.

As you process the responses, you can use your understanding of the left brain, right brain differences, described earlier, to start to narrow down the options. For example:

Gold and Green personalities (left brain dominant) generally ask for facts, and focus the conversation on practicalities, for example details of the solution's technology and implementation process.

Orange and Blue personalities (right brain dominant) will tend to talk more about perceptions and feelings, for example the impact of a solution on their customers and employees.

As you grow to understand your customer more, you will be able to use the more detailed color descriptions provided in Part 2 of this book to home in on the dominant personality style, and in some cases even identify a secondary characteristic.

Asking questions in these general areas helps to reveal a customer's primary personality color. Furthermore, until you know which personality color you are dealing with, it is smart to mostly ask questions and listen to answers, rather than express your own views. Let's look at some typical personality-related responses for each of these questions.

'What is most important to you?'

The idea of asking questions around the topic of 'what is important' is to start to build a picture of what your customer *values*.

If the answer seems to focus around people (impact, feelings, perceptions) you are possibly talking with a Blue.

If the response focuses mostly on financial aspects of the solution, ROI, and the impact on the bottom line to the company, your customer is likely a Gold personality.

If you receive many questions on the technology, details of the functionality, and future impact to the company's direction, that suggests you are dealing with a Green.

If the emphasis is on competitive advantage, gaining market share, and personal career benefits, the customer might be an Orange.

'What do you see as your greatest challenges and top priorities?'

This is another good question area to bring out values, and areas of particular interest and concern.

Basically, a **Blue** is concerned about other people, so Blues will often see their top priority as the well-being of people in the company. They are interested in ways to improve employee morale, and making the employees' jobs less stressful. Another Blue priority is the customer: customer service, customer perception, and customer satisfaction. Blues will tend to view change as more of a challenge than an opportunity, and will be cautious rather than adventurous. Blues can be flexible about their priorities.

A **Gold** is often most concerned about the company's performance and financial priorities. A Gold personality might see the greatest challenge as meeting a timeline or a financial milestone or a company goal. A Gold will prefer to adhere to established processes, and worry about disruption to business-as-usual. Achieving consensus in the management team is another typical Gold concern. Golds will often express their priorities in a clear order and with specific time targets.

A **Green** personality will probably list multiple challenges, possibly with an emphasis on technology. A Green will be interested in finding the best solution to the problem, will look for breakthrough ideas in technology and process, and will want to be convinced that the solution will both solve current problems and meet future needs for the company. You might get responses that include several 'objectively considered' alternative solutions.

Greens typically have informed opinions around technology choices, but will always welcome more information. They will be prepared to take time to come to a firm conclusion. Greens will therefore be flexible about their priorities, and willing to revise ideas based on new information. A typical Green response will be to express concern about integrating a new solution into the existing environment. Basically, Greens are concerned about being right.

An **Orange** personality will express their challenges in more personal terms. Listen to see if an adversary or competitor is identified where the challenge is to win against them. Oranges will worry about convincing others that their recommendations are winners: 'Is there a strong likelihood of success choosing this?' or 'Can this be implemented the quickest?' Oranges often express a strong sense of urgency. The Orange personality type is concerned about being best.

Don't forget that the answers to the 'what is the greatest challenge' question need to be taken in context and alongside

106

the responses to the other questions. If you are talking to someone in a company in severe financial difficulty, about a solution that will allow them to implement a lucrative new product line, don't be surprised if the answer has something to do with revenue generation. Although that can be characterized as a 'Gold' answer, in that situation any color might give you the same response.

'What would your approach be?'

Blues approach a solution by seeking consensus from all that will be involved. They evaluate direction as a team and make their decision as a team.

Golds lay their approach out in a formal plan that includes a schedule leading to the implementation of the solution. Golds issue directives and will delegate assignments to others.

Greens will adopt a thorough approach. They will flag conditionals to watch for and alternative responses to meet these. The Green approach is never cast in concrete.

The **Orange** approach will be easy to understand and most straightforward. Oranges like to go from point A to Z as fast as possible, spending the least amount of effort and expense in the journey.

Observe in context

How a person behaves and reacts to you gives further indications of their personality type.

Blues are warm and friendly and respond warmly to small talk about people and situations. They will try to make you comfortable.

Gold personalities are structured and schedule oriented - typically formal and serious. Golds will take positions of power or dominance; but be aware that different cultures have different indicators of power and dominance.

Greens are succinct in conversation, liking debate and stressing logic. If you ask them about a phone or other new gadget feature, they may respond with a fact or opinion.

Oranges are action-oriented and position themselves as the center of attention. They respond to small talk about sports by engaging with a challenging response.

How someone organizes and holds meetings is a strong indicator of personality type. Gold is formal and aware of time and will express displeasure if promptness is not observed. An Orange might be multi-tasking during the meeting. Blues are not so controlled by time restrictions and can accept approximate start times and extend past stop times. A Green will almost always ask tough questions, often with follow ups based on your answers.

In your first meeting or before, you should discover their title or role in the company. This provides an important clue to their personality, because personality types gravitate to certain types of jobs. It's not a perfect indicator, but a strong clue.

CEO, CFO, COO, and Directors are usually Gold.

Sales VP is usually Orange.

HR is usually Blue.

CIO, Engineering VP, and engineers are usually Green.

How they are dressed will provide additional clues. Gold is traditional and formal, often wearing suits. Orange is trendy casual, polo and golf attire. Blue is fairly casual and fashionable but pays attention to color coordination and artistic style. Green is casual and comfortable, as if fashion doesn't matter. However, remember that people are color spectrums: sometimes a person will dress to their secondary color (or even be dressed by a spouse). A stylish, color-coordinated, but frumpy dresser might be a rare Green-Blue or just a Green with a Blue spouse.

You also can learn personality information from the environment and surroundings where the conversation takes place. Meeting inside their office will provide a wealth of clues; observe the office decoration and contents to learn what they value.

A Blue's office may to have a comfortable artistic look with artwork, music, family pictures, pet pictures and plants. Blue offices are relaxed and are oriented to make the visitor feel comfortable.

The Gold personality will be very organized and fairly neat. Pictures could include symbols of 'Leadership', 'Perseverance', and 'Teamwork'. Books will include popular business best sellers, strategy books, and organizational guides. You will most likely see organization charts, mission and vision statements, and credentials like degrees.

The Green will have more of a practical tech-look possibly with gadgets, scientific themes and technical books. Often the Green office looks cluttered to everyone else, but the Green knows where everything is.

The Orange personality will have family pictures on a vacation, team pictures at company events or memorabilia from their favorite teams, personal trophies from sports and performance plaques. Everything they ordinarily use will be close at hand.

Of course everyone can have a blend in decorating their office, but the central theme can lean towards one of the four personality types.

Narrowing it down

It's usually easy to get the customer down to one of two personality styles, such as when determining left-brain (Gold or Green) or right-brain (Orange or Blue). To further refine your assessment of personality style, here are some subtle differences and similarities that help distinguish which personality style you are addressing.

Golds and Greens are left-brain personalities so they are both good with detail and problem solving. Golds are more structured; while Greens demand their freedom. Golds do not welcome change as Greens do. Golds are better at managing time, while Greens respond to deadlines by working overtime.

Blues and Oranges are right-brain personalities. Both enjoy small talk, interaction with people and a variety of social activities. You can tell them apart because Blues do not enjoy conflict where Oranges will embrace conflict as a personal challenge. Oranges also have a competitive nature; Blues a comforting nature.

Golds and Oranges are bottom-line-driven; concrete thinkers who want quick results. A difference between Golds and Oranges is that Oranges tend to be optimistic and Golds are more cautious. Golds are usually thorough and organized, Oranges rarely so. Oranges live for the moment while Golds are excellent planners. Golds are formal where Oranges tend to be casual. Both prefer to *tell* rather than ask.

Blues and Greens are intuitive thinkers; they seemingly understand something or leap to a conclusion without obvious antecedents in the conversation. They are more inclined to dive deep into a subject than Golds and Oranges. Blues and Greens are both slow to make decisions. A strong difference between Blues and Greens is that Blues like small talk and Greens are very direct in their communication. Greens also like to debate where Blues will avoid debatable topics. Blues will try and make you feel comfortable and

110

Greens are seaming oblivious to your comfort. Both tend to *ask* questions. Blues ask to learn about the person while Greens ask to gain insight and information.

Both Greens and Oranges can appear to be confrontational. However, an Orange is challenging you as a person and potential competitor – but can easily switch to seeing you on their team. A Green is abrupt because what is behind you, your company's products and reputation, is more important to them than who you are. A Green might have trouble remembering your name.

Greens and Oranges enjoy their freedom and don't mind any lack of structure in a meeting. Both can handle debate and thrive and succeed in chaotic situations. However, Greens enjoy detail and Oranges care for more of the big picture. A Green's priority is 'ability' while an Orange's priority is 'performance.' Oranges make decisions impulsively where Greens weigh the alternatives and so are sometimes slower to make decisions – but not always. A very bright Green can leap to a conclusion in an instant with reasoning that is not apparent to others. At other times, the Green already could have experience in the area, ranked the alternatives, and formed their conclusion before the meeting started. A Green will have opinions that seem individual or even strange, while an Orange will have more mainstream likes and dislikes.

Both Golds and Blues will be engaging. But the Blue will be interested in who you are. The Gold will be interested in your status in the business and the community, and how you have performed. A Gold personality will establish that you are a good parent; while a Blue will be interested in what your kids look like.

Blues and Golds like security and safety and will resist change. They like things predictable and consistent. Conflict and chaos make them uncomfortable. The telling difference is that Blues are not as organized and structured as the Gold. A Blue will be relaxed and indifferent to how long the meeting takes. However, time is a priority to the Gold; they will be irritated if the meeting does not end on time. Likewise, when the goals of the meeting are accomplished, the Gold will wish to immediately end the meeting.

Real-life examples

A question I ask in our workshops in relation to identifying people is 'What personality style do you think Tiger Woods is?' Many will say Orange because of his competitive nature. Some will say Gold since he is so disciplined with his work ethic and practice schedule. Actually, the answer is Green. Think about it: who would change his golf swing after winning over fifty golf tournaments and thirteen majors? A Green would! Greens are perfectionists and always try to improve. Tiger is quiet, doesn't really socialize with the crowd and always talks about his golf swing, the hole set ups and his strategy. You can identify him as a left-brain person that is focused on the detail of his golf game.

On the other hand, when I ask what color Phil Mickelson is the answer I get most of the time is Orange – which is correct. Phil is a big time crowd pleaser and a risk taker. Who in their right mind would try to cut the trees on the 18th hole of the US Open in 2006 and lose it with a double bogey? An Orange would. When Phil won the Memorial in 2007, the commentator started to ask him about his game, but Mickelson stopped him in his tracks. Before getting to details, Phil wanted to first acknowledge all the mothers in the audience on Mother's Day. That is a right brain characteristic.

During the final round of the Fed Ex tournament in the fall of 2007, Phil and Tiger were paired up. Phil was up by one stroke as they teed off on the 18th hole. Tiger was perfectly down the middle of the fairway and Phil was further back in the rough. If Phil plays it safe, he should win the hole and the tournament. Tiger gets on the green in two and Phil debates whether to lay up his second shot or go for the green in two. After a few minutes of strategizing with his caddy, Phil pulls

112

out his three-wood and the crowd roars. He's going for the green! He hits it off to the left of the green in the rough and then goes on to win the hole and the tournament. That's how an Orange competes!

Excelling in sports does not indicate an Orange personality. Many excellent athletes are technical competitors – they love the game more than the competition. Greens compete against themselves, Oranges against others. Both like to win because winning validates what they each value, even though what they value is different.

How about Donald Trump, big corporate CEO. Is he Gold or Orange? The answer is Orange. He's a risk taker as shown by his several bankruptcies. He's a showman who started a TV show wrapped around his character rather than concentrating on another real estate deal. Trump is not afraid to 'get in your face' as he did with Rosie O'Donnell. A Gold personality is more cautious in both planning and execution than we see in Trump, and a Gold personality would typically not insult or criticize people publicly. Even though Trump usually appears in a suit, he really does not dress formally so as distinctively. For instance, his hairstyle is distinctly individual. Gold is likely a secondary color for Donald Trump.

Some words that are helpful to associate with each personality style are:

Blue – People and Cooperation

Gold – Process and Completion

Green – Possibilities and Competence

Orange – Performance and Competition.

PART 4. CONNECTING 4
PEOPLE IN SELLING

16. Personality-Based Selling

Every company has its own sales methods and processes. We are not going to define a new sales process for you because you do not have to change your sales process to make use of personality insights to improve your success rate.

No matter how you handle the sales cycle, no matter what products services or solutions you sell, using the Connecting 4 People approach will help you in multiple ways.

As soon as you make contact with your customer, you should identify the key decision makers, and start to build relationships. So, what's new? Now, armed with the knowledge you have acquired about personality styles, you will start to identify the personality type of the key people in the customer's organization, and customize the way you conduct each step of the sales process to make good use of those insights.

The following chapters provide some practical hints for using personality style insights to help you to:

Connect with the customer and build strong customer relationships;

Fine-tune your way of communicating with the customer to match the customer's own personality style;

Understand and make use of different perspectives on needs, value, risk and decision-making;

Anticipate and handle customer objections;

Bring the sales cycle to a successful close with a buying decision.

Understanding your own personality, the personality of others and how these styles interact, will improve your ability in each of these areas. An appreciation of personality styles provides insights into customers' different perspectives on needs, value, risk and decision-making. This casts new light on our sales techniques as we adjust our approach to work with each customer's own unique combination of preferences and attitudes. But this is not a rigid formula. Your customers are still people!

Understanding the customer's personality style will help you increase your chances of *winning the sale* and *shortening the sales cycle*. These are two results every sales leader looks for!

17. Building Customer Relationships

Selling is about persuasion – convincing someone to adopt your point of view. Whether it's convincing your spouse to go to the movies, your son to do their homework or a customer to accept the terms of your proposal, selling is getting someone to *do something*. It's motivating another to take the action you want.

Back in the mid-'80s when I was still new in my sales career I inherited an account from my predecessor in Birmingham, Alabama. Anticipation of my first meeting with this company's president left me a little nervous, because I knew that the most important goal was to establish my credibility and build trust. This customer was the largest in my portfolio but they had the potential to be several times larger. My goal was to triple our business within three years.

During the first couple of months, my customer would test me on how well I could push our corporate teams to meet delivery dates. He kept track of how often I would follow through on his requests. He had me multi-tasking several issues at once. Fortunately, it was natural for me to let him know ahead of time if I couldn't live up to the deadline he wanted.

We had some frustrating moments. Yet after six months of managing this client's issues around deliveries, credit, new technology and future forecasts, we built a long lasting, trusting relationship that tripled his business in the first three years. He knew I cared about his success as much as my own. After one year on the account he offered me my own office in his building. Basically, he knew I worked for him and he didn't have to pay my salary.

I didn't realize what personality style this customer was at the time, but I can look back at how competitive and go-getting he was and realize most likely he was like me, an Orange. His secondary type was probably Gold. Our communication was direct, with no hidden agendas or motives, and I was able to say what was on my mind. He knew I would put his needs before mine each and every time.

You cannot sell effectively without building sound relationships. Customers must know you well enough that they believe what you say, and believe that you have their best interests at heart. Relationships are based on trust, which is developed over time. Trust between two people tends to be built up step by step, with each gradually accumulating more and more trust based on their experience of positive actions and trustworthy behavior.

Trusting someone is associated with how we feel about them and how we predict they will behave. Will they come through for us? Have they been consistent in what they have said and done in the past? And trust is about our own level of confidence: have we done business with them before? The 'trust' factor is more important than anything else. It's even more important than price. People often make decisions when they are emotionally driven by the sales person or their company to do so and a relationship of trust makes it so much easier for the customer to decide.

How can an understanding of the color spectrum help a sales professional to build better relationships? This is neither a trick nor is it a well-defined process. Your growing understanding of the personality styles and the temperament of each of the personalities will help you in several ways, for example:

You will find that you learn about your customer's values and preferences much more quickly. This will enable you to relate more easily and in a more meaningful way.

Your new appreciation of the potential contribution of different personality styles will make you more readily

120

accepting of differences and better able to communicate with empathy.

You will discover that you will adjust your own behaviors and attitudes to more closely align with those of your customer. This will aid communication and establish trust more quickly.

Don't think of this as a mechanical process. Use the approach to help you relate to the customer, to fine-tune your communication style, to empathize and to build relationships. Sales success will follow naturally.

18. COMMUNICATING WITH THE CUSTOMER

We all must *connect* with other people in both our personal life and business life. Good communication helps us connect with others. Poor communication leads to lack of comprehension and lack of trust which in turn makes it much more difficult to build a strong relationship. If a Gold real estate agent says to a Green house-seeker: 'I know how important location is,' we now know there is a significant chance they could misunderstand each other! Think back to the last time you and your spouse or partner disagreed over a purchase. Was it the item that was the problem? Or were you each placing different values and expectations from the potential purchase? Let's look at how personalities can color communication.

Communication is always two-way; it involves both talking and listening. A rule-of-thumb for sales persons is that your customers should always be allowed to talk more than you! The person that talks the most is usually least in control. Make it your goal to let the customer do at least 60% of the talking in a discussion. The more the customer says, the more we find out. It's almost that simple, but not quite.

We still need to correctly hear the *entirety* of what the customers are saying: what they intend to say, and what they unconsciously communicate by how they say it. We need to listen for two components: What is said (the facts), and how it's said (the feelings.)

Each of the four personality types communicates differently. More than just the words they say, each approaches a conversation differently. The personalities of those involved in a conversation can affect not just what is said but also: the pace and tempo of the conversation; the intimacy of the conversational style; whether the conversation stays on track or wanders; whether the tone becomes argumentative or amicable.

By listening carefully, we can gather clues about the personality types involved in any meeting or conversation.

Style of communication

When we listen carefully, we can make a good guess which personality group our conversationalist belongs to. This is important because we cannot just administer the Connecting 4 People Assessment to everyone we meet! Knowing their personality type, we can respond with what someone in that color group would naturally expect. We can pace our conversational responses to their expectations, making them more at ease. By adjusting our pace and responding as they expect, we build trust; 'She really understands me,' or 'He is one of us!'

Here is what to expect in communications style from each of the personalities, Blue, Gold, Green, and Orange.

Blues enjoy small talk. Typically, there is no sense of urgency when a Blue is in conversation about something personal such as friends, family or a hobby. Blues will ask questions about you; they are interested in your answer. Blues have no trouble sharing a conversation, even if another person is talking more. Blues demonstrate sincere interest in what is happening in the life of their conversationalist. For Blues, developing trusting relationships is paramount and this is apparent in the way they communicate.

Blues like the conversation to keep flowing and can talk about anything and everything. In fact, sometimes it seems that getting to closure on the conversation is not of much interest to a Blue. When talking with a Blue customer, make sure you have good eye contact. Blues are the best at reading body language. They listen to *how* something is said not just simply *what* is said. Blues do not enjoy arguing or debate; it is

124

best to avoid conversations where there might be strong confrontational opinions.

Golds are more formal in their discussion. Golds always prefer to have an agenda when going into a meeting. I've actually have put together an agenda for a twenty-minute meeting that had just three words on it – Introduction, Discussion, Close – and the Gold client was pleased to see it! Setting expectations for a sales meeting is very important to a Gold. What is the purpose of the meeting and what do we expect to accomplish? There must be a purpose and reason for meeting. Make sure that if you have a set time for a meeting, you end the meeting promptly when the time is up. A Gold expects a forty-five-minute meeting to last forty-five minutes. If the meeting looks like it might run over, ask the customer if they would like to finish the meeting or would they prefer to continue. This will gain credibility with the Gold.

Golds don't like it when they feel their time is being wasted. Starting a meeting with small talk is acceptable only until they signal the meeting has begun. So keep the small talk brief and get to your agenda. Keep your conversation moving and be concrete. Expect tough questions on the impact of your products and services on company performance. Golds need a *reason* to buy. Golds respect those who follow through on what they say they promise. Following up the meeting in writing in an email or a letter will give you credibility and earn the Gold's respect.

Greens communicate by asking many questions across a range of topics. Expect your most challenging questions from Greens. Keep your conversation succinct with a Green and get right down to business. Small talk is not appropriate unless the customer initiates it. With Greens, conversations typically are inquisitive, including many questions about: the features of the products and services; how these will integrate into the business; and how these might be part of their business evolution going forward. Greens like to discuss and debate, often playing the devil's advocate.

Greens are visionary and always looking to the future. They can talk on the 'big picture' level and then immediately dive into the details. Greens will test you if they have the chance, sometimes to display their knowledge and sometimes to establish your credibility. Many times it feels as though there is a lot of resistance with a Green because the questions never seem to end. But questions are to be expected from a Green; this doesn't necessarily mean you are not making progress. If you are fielding these questions correctly, then you are, in fact, making progress in the Green's mind. When you do not know an answer, or are unsure of your answer, tell a Green firmly that you'll come back later with an answer. For a Green, that's much better than giving a fuzzy or evasive answer.

Orange personalities are entertainers; they love to be the center of attention. I sometimes joke: 'When I'm done talking about me, I'll let you talk about me'! Let the Orange customer talk as much as they want. It's frustrating to an Orange when they do not get the chance to express themselves. Then this frustration can come out as a competitive challenge to your propositions. Small talk is expected and can range from family activities to sporting events to vacations.

Oranges are optimistic and high energy. Keep the conversation moving and active. Get them involved, excited and interested as soon as you can or you might lose them! Oranges are tough to pin down, because they multi-task and stay very active. Oranges are impulsive and live for the immediate moment. More than others they live on the edge – you must try to keep close to this edge too!

Calling on the Blue customer

Sitting down with a Blue customer is likely to be a pleasant experience because Blues are generally warm and friendly. Expect the conversation to flow naturally. Blue customers will want to get to know you and they will also ask questions about you. Expect a lot of personal discussion around family and relationships. When talking about their organization they will focus on the needs of the people. If they trust you they will open up more than any of the other personalities.

Avoid controversy with Blues, as they are not comfortable with conflict. Eye contact and body language are important since this is what they are best at reading. Honesty is paramount with a Blue. Blues will try to hide any discomfort they might have with the sales process because they don't like to offend. You must help them overcome this by asking them how they feel about each step of the process. Express *your* feelings and then pause with body language that solicits *their* feelings.

Blues are not very interested in technical details and specifications. Most important to Blues is how your product or service will impact the people and the organization and how it will improve their environment. In a meeting with the buyer's decision team, the Blue will often be more attentive to the group than to you, the seller. Let them bond with the group if the group is reacting favorably to you. If the group is unifying against you, directly engage the Blue with a reason the group should feel differently. Then, let the Blue convince them to change.

When it comes time to ask a Blue for a commitment to move forward, do not be aggressive; use a soft close asking something along the lines of, 'What would you like to see for the next step.' Blues are generally warm and friendly – but don't take their attitude for granted, at least not until you have built a close and trusting relationship. Blues are not be as aggressive negotiators as the other personalities. When they negotiate it will often be around the people aspects of your solution. You should counter with similar people-oriented characteristics of your product or service.

When meeting with Blues.

Maintain eye contact

Listen with empathy

Build a relationship

Use both verbal and nonverbal expression

Feel free to speak figuratively

Focus on people topics.

Calling on the Gold customer

A Gold personality is likely to be the final decision maker or to approve the decisions of others.

Golds dress more formally so wearing a suit will never be a bad move when calling on a Gold. Expect the Gold customer to take control of the meeting. Come in with an agenda and be prepared for a formal discussion with pertinent questions about your products and services. Punctuality is very important with Gold. When you start the meeting, check with the customer that you still have the allotted time for the meeting as previously scheduled. You might find that your time has been cut down. If they want the meeting to run over the time, thank them for the additional opportunity. Keep an eye on your time and stick to the agenda. If the Gold departs from the agenda, accept this, meet their immediate interest, and then return in a businesslike way to the original agenda.

Golds do not like surprises. Set the expectations for the meeting and keep the flow moving forward. Golds like checkpoint summaries as you discuss each topic and this is a good time to ask for questions. Allow time in your schedule planning for the Gold to ask questions; frequently they will have these prepared beforehand. Golds are patient listeners

128

and are interested to hear your comments and responses. However, this does not mean they are agreeing with your answers. Golds tend to keep their thoughts to themselves and often wear a poker face for meetings. So you must specifically ask for their buy-in: 'Do you agree?' or 'Does this meet your expectations?'

It is important to Golds that you understand their business pain. Golds want to know: what problem your service will resolve; why this is important; how they will benefit; and what it will cost them in money, time, and internal effort. Golds also understand that the sales process is also one of building a trusted relationship. Golds like to follow a structured buying process, making sure all the i's are dotted and the t's are crossed as the process unfolds.

If you're not a Gold yourself, and you get off on the wrong footing with a Gold personality, you may find it very difficult to re-engage. Try bringing in a similarly ranked Gold from your own company. Establish the agenda and then just act as a facilitator to the meeting. Let the two Golds engage and work together – they know how to deal with these situations.

Golds need a reason to buy so financial incentives are beneficial. Be prepared to explain your product or service's financial impact on your client's company. Golds will negotiate on the financial aspects of the deal such as return on investment, warranty, and terms and conditions of the contract.

If all the objectives of the meeting have been accomplished, state this and ask to end the meeting. 'That's all I have on the agenda, I know your time is valuable, shall we adjourn until next time?' You can close the Gold with a checkpoint query: 'Have we reached an understanding here?' Then 'Do you agree we are ready to proceed?'

When meeting with **Golds**:

Be direct and professional

Track the time

Stay on task

Use direct language

Use correct and proper language

Pay attention to etiquette.

Calling on the Green customer

Greens can make or break a sale in short order. A Green is usually present at a sales meeting because the Green is the expert that the actual decider of the purchase trusts. Prepare for a meeting with a Green customer by researching background information. Visit their web site and understand their business in as much detail as possible. Being an Orange, I have a natural tendency to just 'wing it.' That once got me in trouble at a meeting with a Green customer who challenged my lack of preparation. Expect Greens to have researched your company and its products and services. They will sometimes email questions beforehand, and when this occurs, come prepared with answers. If they ask something you do not know, do not guess; simply say 'I will need to get back to you on that. Is next week OK or do you need the answer sooner?'

Greens typically don't enjoy the sales process. They find it bearable when it is to acquire something they specifically need, or the quality of the solution is a matter of professional pride, or someone they hope to impress asks for their opinion. Otherwise the meeting is likely to be viewed as an intrusion of their time. Be careful not to bore Greens. When bored they can become argumentative or test you with particularly difficult questions. Telling them what they already know is a recipe for trouble.

130

Greens are uncomfortable with socializing and small talk and may not even recognize it as such. For example, a simple opening question such as 'How are you today?' might be answered with a moment of detached thought and then a literal answer about their health and current attitude. At other times, small talk might divert the Green into an entirely new line of questioning which has nothing to do with your agenda. You should get right to the purpose of your meeting unless the Green clearly wants to chat about something that is of interest to them.

Greens do not mind getting into a debate with sales people and you should expect the toughest questions from them. They see their role in the meeting as establishing the quality and credibility of: the product or service, your company (their supplier), and you as a person. Sometimes Greens already know the answers to some of the questions they fire off. This could simply be a test of your ability or knowledge, or the Green may feel it necessary to prove to peers or management that they are on top of the situation. Sometimes the appropriate response in this sticky situation is to reply: 'My CTO would love to discuss this with you. Can I set up a call where you can explore this in detail?'

An aggressive Orange calling on a passive Green, presents opportunities for misunderstanding and derailment of the meeting and the sale. In this case, tone down any rhetoric or challenge and complement them on their knowledge and standing in the field. Play the 'get back to them with details' card. This is a case where the Orange wins by calling a time out.

Greens are not persuaded by style or panache. Socializing in a sales situation is not of value to them. They're interested in the facts, the technology and what your products and services can do for them now and in the future. Don't pressure the Green to close, since they will not decide until all their questions are answered and their objections countered. It may seem like they are slow, but in fact, they decide quickly once the reach their information comfort threshold. It only seems they are slow to make decisions from your perspective, not to them.

It may seem like a Green is negotiating on the capability and functionality of the solution when they compare it to other offerings; most often this is their internal way to reach a comfortable, accurate ranking of the choices before them. Once a Green decides, it is very difficult to change their mind. Arguments or negotiation will not do this, only bringing up a fact or circumstance that was not present in their original calculation.

On closing the meeting, ask Greens if they have any outstanding questions. Express your willingness to work on getting them the answers they need. Greens need a lot of information, so expect them to follow up with email and other questions after the initial meeting. When selling to Greens it is a good move to follow up each meeting with an email containing supplemental documents and asking if they need more information.

When meeting with **Greens**:

Expect many questions

Give them time to think

Be succinct

Be factual

Be logical.

Calling on the Orange customer

Oranges enjoy being the customer. You can expect a fast-moving and engaging conversation with an Orange. Let them speak the most since they love to be the center of attention.

Small talk is expected; often it will cover sports, their team at work, or their viewpoints on any number of popular issues. Oranges like to be stroked for their achievements, so play to that. Oranges might multi-task even during a conversation. If their phone rings, expect them to answer it. Then multi-task yourself until they finish – this takes off the pressure and establishes you as a peer.

Don't get into a lot of detail. Oranges like the big picture and prefer the cliff notes version of the pitch. Include discussion about the immediate benefits of your product and services. Indirectly explore how this solution will make them look good in their organization. Oranges are somewhat prone to fads and seek peer esteem, which manifests in an appreciation for the latest, the greatest and the fastest things on the market.

Oranges are bottom-line driven and look for the best deal possible. Flexibility is important to Oranges; it gives them room to maneuver. They will want to get your solution as soon as possible as they are also impatient to get it done and get on to the next competition.

Oranges enjoy being tagged with the responsibility for the close of the sale so expect them to negotiate for the best deal. Negotiating is a competitive game to Oranges – so expect a tough negotiation! Oranges as negotiators aim to 'win' the negotiation; this might prolong reaching an agreement better served through compromise. Engage the Orange's natural good sportsmanship to bring negotiating to a close at a point when everyone's ahead.

When meeting with **Oranges**:

Talk in concrete terms

Provide the big picture, not too much detail

Be energetic

133

Be direct

Encourage interaction

Be entertaining, but not more entertaining than your customer.

The business/social balance

I'm often asked, 'How do the different personality types view client entertainments?' Well, each person has his or her own entertainment preferences and attitudes to socializing.

Can you tell who will be open to socializing and who will not? For the most part, the left-brain personalities (Gold and Green) are more objective and would prefer business first. The right-brained Blue and Orange, being more subjective, should be more open to entertainment as a way to break the ice before getting down to business. Entertainment should never be an exchange of favors, but Greens and Golds might need to be assured that there is nothing expected in return.

While tastes vary, the Blue personality usually enjoys dinners and social settings that include plays, music and the arts. The Orange personality is more apt to lean towards sporting events such as golf tournaments and ball games. Green personalities will also enjoy the arts but might only accept an invitation after you have gained credibility. Golds will also accept an invitation, but usually after you demonstrate follow through by meeting prior commitments.

When it comes to building a relationship, which should come first, socializing or business? Should you ask for a business meeting to discuss goals or needs first; or can you start with by inviting them to the theater or a golf game? I have met clients for the first time by inviting them to a golf tournament and the relationship developed perfectly well from a first contact in this informal environment. While these clients welcomed the informal meeting, others might never accept an entertainment invitation without first meeting you in a business setting.

They key with entertainment is *not* to use it as a means to convince customers to buy your products and services, but more as a means of building a relationship.

19. WHY DO CUSTOMERS BUY?

Why do customers buy?

What a great question. The answer is complicated, and never black and white. Customers are people, and people are sometimes unpredictable and awkward. That is why the business of selling is so interesting, challenging and worthwhile!

A customer starts the buying process with both *business reasons*, and *personal reasons* to seek a new product or service. Their assessment of value is colored by both *logic* and *emotion*, as is their assessment of risk. Their ultimate selection of a product or service involves both *objective* and *subjective* factors.

While we can never hope to predict the behavior of everyone with absolute certainty, the use of the assessment can help by providing valuable clues to likely behaviors and attitudes. But for this to be useful we need to understand how the different colors perceive needs, assess value, view risk and weigh up their options.

How personality type influences buying decisions

The customer's buying process usually starts off with a perceived *need*. Different personality types have different perspectives on needs and will prioritize their needs differently.

The different perspectives on need are linked to different ways of establishing *value*. Something that is important and attractive to one personality type may be uninteresting to another.

136

Different personality types view *risk* differently. Outside the business world, this is obvious: not everyone likes to bungee jump.

Different people use different kinds of criteria to make up their minds when presented with options. For each personality type these are consistently linked to their attitudes to value and risk.

Clearly, your customer's personality style is the key to understanding how they prefer to make decisions to buy. If you have insights into how the different personality color types relatively weight needs, value, risk, and decision criteria, you will be better prepared to engage with them in a way that will influence their decision to buy – from you!

Needs

Selling is largely about understanding and meeting the *needs* of the customer. When customers perceive a need, that's when they start thinking about buying something!

As you might expect by now, each of the different personality types tends to have a different perspective on what their most important needs are, and therefore what they value most. Also, as I mentioned earlier, customers have both personal needs and business needs.

Understanding your customers' personality styles will help you to understand whether personal needs or business needs will carry more weight when they make important decisions. It will also give you insights into *which* business needs and *which* personal needs are at the front of their mind.

Once you understand their personality style, you can select and communicate the appropriate benefits that best match their real needs. You must color the solution according to their needs, so that they take action and buy from you. Needs are directly related to what the customer values. It's all about connecting with what is most important to them and not what is important to you.

Business needs

At the beginning of the customer's buying process, there exists an identified *business need* within the buying company. Customers purchase products and solutions to impact specific factors in their business model or to reach specific business goals. Some typical examples are:

Increase profits and revenue;

Reduce operational costs;

Increase productivity;

Improve cash flow;

Reduce inventory;

Improve customer satisfaction;

Reduce product defect rates;

Reduce whole life total cost of ownership of equipment;

Bring new products to market faster;

Open new markets for products.

It is typical of a business need that it is tangible, and that it is possible to set *objective criteria* to decide whether the need has been met. If the business need is to lower product defect rates, the customer can measure the rate today and set a numerical target for improvement – say, 40% reduction in defective products.

Business needs are also openly expressed. The customer does not keep it a secret that, for example, the reason they need a new order handling system is to improve customer service performance.

Being open and honest about a need makes in easy for the sales person to try to satisfy the customer. But, as we'll see, customers aren't always candid about their needs.

Personal needs

Alongside the stated business needs, there may be one or more *personal needs* that will also affect the buyer's assessment of your offering. For example:

Will this product make life easier for me and for my team?

Will I get a promotion or a bonus if it turns out well?

How will I be viewed by 'xxx' in making this decision?

Will my subordinates be grateful and stop giving me a hard time?

Will this help me achieve my personal sales target?

It is very important that a sales person should know if a personal factor is likely to influence the decision, one way or another. There is no surefire way of uncovering this knowledge.

However, if you use your understanding of personality styles to help build relationships with the customer decision-makers, and with other people in the customer's organization, then you stand a much better chance of being seen as an insider and share in that less public information. If you are going to help your customer, you need to know their *real* needs.

What people value

As I pointed out earlier, there is a difference between the characteristics of the left brain colors (Green and Gold) and the right brain (Orange and Blue), and this becomes clear when we consider what each personality type values most.

Although it's risky to generalize too much, left-brain people tend to be more logical and objective as they consider value, and right-brain people tend to rely more on emotion and subjective impressions. But even objective thinkers have emotions, and emotional people can understand logic too.

Here are some examples of what different personality types tend to value most highly when considering a business purchase:

The Blue personality values how the solution or service would impact customer satisfaction, employee morale and relationships.

The Gold personality values what the return on investment would be, how it would increase revenues, reduce costs, improve productivity, improve cash flow or manage inventory more efficiently.

The Green personality values how this would impact technology improvements, efficiencies and effectiveness within the organization.

The Orange personality values beating the competition, improving performance and gaining market share.

Even in a non-business purchase, the differences in perspectives on 'what is important' can be dramatic. In our Competitive Excellence workshops, I have learned a lot from my real estate clients about the widely different needs and attitudes to value that are brought into play when people are buying a new house.

140

Blues want their house to be warm and welcoming. They are attracted by good design and attractive craftsmanship. They want the house to be in a safe neighborhood, among people like themselves.

To **Golds** the financial investment is important: they will focus on the house's condition, potential resale value, and financing. They already know exactly what type of layout they want for the house. If it's four thousand square feet, downstairs master bedroom, three additional bedrooms, three baths, and backyard pool enclosed by a wrought iron fence, then nothing else will do!

Greens are concerned about the practicality of the floor plan, the condition of a house and how energy efficient it is. How well constructed is the house? Is the heating and air-conditioning equipment in good condition? What warranties are in place and what is the value of the home?

Oranges look for a home that works well for entertainment and socializing. They're also attracted by unique amenities in the home, and a building that's easy to run and maintain. An Orange also wants to know: 'Can I negotiate a great deal?'

Recognizing our own value biases

An eye-opening exercise in our training workshop concerns 'what you think your customer values'. This exercise is done in teams where each team is one of the four personality colors. We ask participants to put themselves in their customer's shoes with the question: 'Imagine you are the customer and evaluating your (real) company for a project, rank in order from most important to the least the top four reasons for doing business with your firm.'

The table on the next page contains the actual answers given during a workshop session for one of our clients, a telecommunications consulting firm.

The answers are clustered according to the personality type of the team that provided the answers.

Blue Team Answers	**Gold** Team Answers
Good communication	Knowledge
Complementary skills	Meeting deliverable dates
Complementary personalities	Flexibility, dealing with ambiguity, adaptability
Creativity	Interpersonal skills
Green Team Answers	**Orange** Team Answers
Free thought	Required expertise
Correct, on spec, on time	Commitment to the client
Flexibility	Competitive price
Quality of product	Capability

The results of this exercise are crucial to understanding the values of each personality. Even though answers are never identical, we find there is a consistency in the responses every time we do it: each color group is naturally inclined to list the items they themselves value. For example, the Blues' perspective on what their customer would value is heavily slanted towards Blue personality characteristics.

Sometimes, as in this real world example, secondary personality characteristics will trickle up, particularly when a participant is nearly balanced between primary and secondary colors. We see this in the Green response 'on time', which is more typical of a Gold. Secondary characteristics are important.

Much the same occurs when we ask teams of real estate agents to go through the same exercise. Most often each color starts with 'location.' This has already been drummed into them during basic agent training. But a closer look reveals that 'location' has a different emotional meaning, and visual association, for all four personalities. A word may have a dictionary definition yet also connote different associations for different personalities.

For the Blue, 'location' has a social dimension and means the 'neighborhood'. For the Orange, it's a house that is convenient to shopping and quick access to major roads. For the Gold, it's a prestigious neighborhood and close to the office. For the Green, it's convenient access to work and school.

This exercise reminds everyone that sellers often assume – wrongly – that their customers share their own values and preferences. Therefore:

You need to adjust your value pitch away from your own values towards those of your customers.

You should be able to draw from your minor color characteristics, to help identify and project what your customer would most desire – assuming you know the personality styles of the decision-makers you are targeting.

Attitudes towards risk

When it comes to making a decision, each personality has to weigh the risk associated with the decision. Each of the colors has a different view of risk, which affects how they will make a decision.

Some people will be satisfied with a small gain in return for a low risk of loss, while another personality will shoot for the moon knowing the losses can be greater.

That's why it's quite common to see the Orange personality go into the relatively high-risk career of sales where there is the potential for huge commissions.

Blues are typically risk averse. Blues prefer security and safety. For Blues risk is directly related to organizational or social change. If we make this decision, will it be the right one for the people in the organization? What are the chances of failure? Is it a safe decision? Does it feel right?

Blues like to hear and then come to believe that the chance of failure is small or, preferably, zero. You need to establish trust and give the Blue customer constant support to move forward. You need to be there for them.

Golds, being left brain, will be logical in their approach. Golds will only take a risk after they analyze the situation and weigh the benefits carefully against the likely return. Golds make prudent decisions after assessing how the result of the decision will impact the organization and the company. What is the return if the risk is taken? Does the potential good outweigh the chances of failure and its impact?

Golds need a lot of valid reasons to make a significant change because Golds view change as disruptive to the day-to-day operation of the organization. Golds also value security and safety. There must be an objective, solid return for taking the risk.

Greens will analyze the situation and if it makes logical sense they will often take a risk. For the Green personality, change is invigorating. 'If we can improve something, we must!'

Being left-brained, Greens will make logical decisions using their ability to assess information and apply logic. Greens are more likely to be mathematically trained and therefore will see risk as quantifiable. For these Greens, risk is expressed as a probability and sometimes as a decision tree.

144

The salesperson should be prepared to present objective evidence based analysis of the risk associated with making the decision compared to the risk associated with not making the decision.

Oranges thrive on risk, and welcome change. They do not see the potential downside; they see the opportunity for upside. Oranges enjoy the freedom of having many possible outcomes. They get excited when there are many different factors they can leverage in a business situation; risk is less important than the opportunity to influence the outcome.

Oranges are optimistic by nature so if they think they can win by taking on risk they usually will. Being impulsive by nature, Oranges typically spend only a short amount of time analyzing a situation. Give them the immediate benefits of making the potential decision and they are on their way!

A good example of how different personality styles view risk can be seen in how they approach investing in the stock market.

Blues might invest for social impact and because the company is humane, moral, or environmentally green; but otherwise they will avoid risk by buying CDs and other stable government-backed investments.

Greens are more likely to be 'value investors' or to follow a chart-based 'technical model' of investing. They also tend to invest in what they know best such as a familiar technology or an industry they work in.

Golds tend to make more conservative long-term investments and would never invest in a volatile and risky stock. It would be common for the Gold to purchase a CD or tax free municipal bonds.

On the other hand, **Oranges** don't mind going for the home run, fully aware that their investment is high risk but

145

with potentially high reward. It is not unusual to see an Orange take the risk on a highly volatile stock in the technology market.

Matching the value proposition to the customer's needs and personality

All sales people have in their heads a set of value propositions for all of their products, services and solutions.

Based on our understanding of personality styles, we now know that different personality types see needs differently and value things differently. This means that we should forget the old idea that there can be one value proposition for a particular product or service. A value proposition is a selling tool, and the value expressed must resonate with the individual customer to whom it's presented.

Since customers vary widely in their estimation of value then we must recognize that *each customer contact might need a new value proposition.*

Moreover, in some cases – selling a complex solution to a large corporation, for example – several key people may have a say in the purchasing decision. For a project like that, you may have to produce a slightly different version of your value pitch for each decision-maker.

This is not always easy. However, an understanding of the personality types provides you with a structure and guidance as to how to do this.

In a selling situation, the value assessment that matters is the assessment of the buyer, and that will vary with the buyer's personality color group. Knowing potential customers' values and needs helps you position the benefits of your products and services in a way that will resonate most with their personality styles, giving you a better chance of moving the sale forward.

146

Decisions, decisions

When the time arrives, what criteria will each of the colors use to finally make a decision? Now that we understand the way in which each color perceives needs, value, and risk, we are starting to form a fairly clear picture of the ways that different people can move to one decision rather than another.

However, there is one more perspective on decision-making that is important to understand, and this too is influenced by personality. Some people have a tendency to make decisions largely on the basis of objective criteria. Others prefer to come to a decision that is more subjective. Most people have elements of both objectivity and subjectivity in their make-up, but the balance varies.

To be *objective* is to attempt to eliminate emotion and bias from a decision. Of course, we are people, not machines, so we never reach pure objectivity. Nevertheless, in business decision-making, the aim is usually to decide on a course of action that can be seen by everyone to be rational.

Subjective refers to our desires and emotions, relationships and accumulated experiences. Being subjective is to be distinctly personal in the consideration of factors: how does it affect me, and those I care about? Sometimes one is aware of subjective influences and sometimes they are unconscious parts of our life. A subjective factor comes from the particular state we are in and the relationships to those around us. Everyone understands that subjective factors are personal, and can therefore vary widely in intensity and importance from person to person.

If you are dealing with a *left-brain* personality type (Green or Gold) the decision will more often lean towards the objective, business aspects of your solution. Business needs will over-ride the personal needs. However, if you are dealing with a *right-brain* decision maker (Blue or Orange), the subjective, personal needs can outweigh the business needs.

Common criteria weighed by the purchasing team when making a decision to buy a product, service or solution are: cost, capability, quality, and after-sales service.

Cost is the total cost of ownership (TCO) including the return on the investment. This cost includes the immediate price, the deferred downstream costs such as maintenance and service, and indirect costs such as any warranties involved.

Capability encompasses the features and functionality of the product or service and the technology that's used. 'What is the product or service able to do?'

Quality is linked to the reliability and longevity of your product. 'Will it last?' 'Will it have problems?' 'Will it consistently perform as promised?'

Service is how well you will take care of the customer if problems arise. 'What hours are you available?' 'What is your response time?' Service is all about your company's attitude on customer care and your ability to perform when issues arise.

Each of these factors – cost, capability, quality, service – is measurable (and therefore able to be assessed *objectively*). However, what determines whether, for example, what level of quality justifies a particular level of cost? Even the most rigorous cost-benefit analysis may contain some subjective judgments. Without that type of formal rigor, we find in practice that each of the four personality styles, as they consider the solution you are offering, will give a different weighting to each of these factors, and that weighting may often be arrived at *subjectively*. Typically:

Blues – give most weight to high **quality** and reliable **service**

148

Golds – focus on highest **quality** for the lowest **cost**.

Greens – want **capability** as well as **quality.**

Oranges – like low **cost** and attentive after-sales **service**.

These preferences reflect the value priorities of each personality style. To further complicate matters, additional preferences may come into play such as the following:

Blues – will take into account the **impact on people** and **aesthetic appeal**

Golds – will favor a solution that offers **stability** and **order**

Greens – seek **novelty** and **interest** in a solution

Oranges – will give extra weight to a solution that boosts **competitiveness;** being **up-to-date and cool** appeals to an Orange too.

We can see that just about any buying decision takes place in a rich and complex environment of varying perspectives on need, different concepts of value, a range of attitudes to risk, and different objective and subjective criteria for selecting a winner.

Even buying something apparently straightforward can involve a complex mixture of different motives. Let's go back to the simple example of a gas barbeque grill that we used earlier.

A **Blue** personality will take into account build quality, safety and the dealer's maintenance and support service. A Blue would also be influenced by an attractive appearance, and might also be interested in fuel efficiency, to minimize environmental impact.

For the **Gold**, buying the grill needs to be a sound investment. The gold will aim for the best quality at a reasonable cost and will tend to buy from a well-known and reputable brand-name company. The Gold will be attracted by a familiar and understandable layout, and by a unit that is and looks solid.

The **Green** will research the investment and look into all the options: propane or natural gas, steel or ceramic grills, paint or stainless steel. A Green must have something that is well-engineered and rich with features.

The **Orange** wants a bargain, but might also pay for the convenience of a service contract. An Orange is interested in quick results: the grill will be easy to install, and easy to ignite and operate. The Orange's grill must look good!

Now that you understand that each personality style goes about making decisions in a different way, you should be prepared to adjust your approach and strategy with each customer based on your understanding of that customer's personality style. If there are multiple decision makers, you can emphasize the aspects of value that will be important to each personality style involved – thereby covering all your bases.

20. Handling Customer Objections

Objections are normal

Many sales professionals fear customer objections. But objections are normal and, if constructively handled, allow you to build stronger customer relationships. It is inevitable that in every sales situation there will be objections at some point in the sales process. Objections simply mean the customer is thinking of all possibilities as they consider your solution. Importantly, it also means you have their attention (a critical step) and they are interested in engaging in a dialogue (a critical next step).

Now you can work toward framing the discussion. So expect and welcome the opportunity to move the sale forward by responding to the objections as they are raised. Of course you must be prepared to respond confidently and effectively, in a manner tuned to their personality style.

Handling customer objections properly builds strong momentum toward success. While some sales training programs believe that objections can be completely prevented, I see objections as an opportunity to dialogue with the customer. The negative effects of customer objections can be minimized by focusing on the needs of the customer – and specifically, not pushing features that may not be relevant to the customer's needs.

You are selling to a person. Acknowledge and then respond to the objections raised by the customer; but in doing so, take their personality type into account. Use this information to adapt your communication style and messages to best convey the benefits of your solution relative to the customer's business and personal needs.

The Five A's

There are **five A's** involved in handling objections: **Anticipate**, **Acknowledge**, **Address**, **Alleviate**, and obtain **Acceptance**.

Just as customers' base decisions on both their personal needs, and their business needs, customer objections also come in two types – **factual objections** and **emotional objections**. The tendency to raise factual objections or to raise more emotional objections is part of personality style. Depending on the personality style of the customer, you can **anticipate** and prepare for objections, which stem from what each personality style values. With anticipation you may be able to remove any grounds for objection completely, so actual objections do not arise. But if an objection does still arise, you will be better prepared to handle it.

Whether a customer's objection is factual or emotional, you need to address the objection to move the sale forward. First, you need to **acknowledge** the customer's concern. You can do that by simply stating: 'I hear what you are saying', 'I understand', or 'I see'. You do not need to agree with the customer, but simply acknowledge that you have heard their concern.

Next you need to **address** the objection. If it's a factual objection you must try to refocus or redirect the customer back to their most important need, which will hopefully outweigh the objection in terms of importance. If the objection is emotional you must clarify or prove to the customer that their concern is not a valid one or they should not have the concern.

Specific circumstances, mood, and outside influences might determine specific customer responses. Your goal is to provide answers to these objections tailored to the personality styles of the buyers. Generate emotions in the customer. Aim to satisfy their personal needs, which reinforce the customer's desire to pick your solution. Likewise, reinforce the idea that your product supports the business need, as weighted in importance by the specific personality type.

Your discussion with the customer will usually make it clear if you have addressed the concern in a way that is satisfactory to the customer. However, don't just assume that everything is resolved: you must ask for **acceptance.** 'Are you satisfied with our answer to your concern?' If you don't ask for acceptance the customer likely will return to the same concern later in the sales process.

If the customer replied 'Yes', you can consider the objection to be **alleviated** and it is unlikely to be brought up again.

Different personalities, different objections

Let's take a look at the sort of objections that you can typically expect from each of the personality types.

With the **Blue** personality expect more emotional objections relating to how the products or services will impact people's jobs, employee morale, and customer satisfaction. Objections are related to people and relationships.

'I'm not sure the rest of the team will be comfortable with this proposal.'

'This will really make our service reps unhappy.'

With the **Gold** personality expect more factual objections related to the financial aspects of the solution. Golds will evaluate the numbers in your proposals with care and raise questions to establish credibility.

'Your ROI won't meet our investment criteria.'

'This looks like it will have a negative impact on our bottom line.'

'I just don't see how the productivity gains will be enough to pay for this.'

With the **Green** personality, expect factual objections around the capability of the solution, the technical aspects, the functionality, and where the solution might fit in to the overall technology strategy down the road.

'I think your competitor has a more advanced technical solution.'

'I just don't think you can achieve the advertised performance using this approach.'

'I'm not sure that your company will be around to support this solution in five years.'

The **Orange** personality is a tough negotiator and places emphasis on the process of buying. They want to raise objections. Oranges also want to know the immediate benefits. Emotional objections are common for the Orange personality. Oranges like to negotiate since they view this as a competitive game.

'I don't think you've tried hard enough with this discount.'

'I'm disappointed you didn't offer us as good a deal as you offered your competitor.'

'I don't see how this will improve our competitive edge.'

Facing facts

Factual objections are just that: they are a fact that must be dealt with. Facts tend to be more important to those that

154

are left brain, **Greens** and **Golds**. Factual objections are often about the numbers. 'Your price is over our budget.' 'The return on investment is short of our expectations.' 'The terms and conditions need to include a three-year warranty.' Factual objections must be addressed head on since they may point out where your products or services are missing the mark in a certain area.

Accept that a factual objection is *valid* from the customer's point-of-view. Factual objections need to be dealt with head on, but do not contradict the customer directly or tell the customer 'you are wrong.' Instead, leverage the personality-style weighted importance of business needs. As we mentioned earlier, a very useful question we can ask a customer at the start of a sales call is 'When it comes to investing in (the product or service) what is most important to you?' This will give you a good indication of their personality style. Now use this knowledge to *redirect* the objection with your response. Refocus the conversation or written answer back to the values that are important to that customer.

For example, if you have already discovered that the most important thing to a customer when buying a computer is storage space and speed, then an objection about price needs to be redirected back to the need for storage space and speed. 'It's worth extra for superior performance and storage. For these features you are getting the best price available.' Consistency is important to Greens and Golds. Remembering their prior answer about relative importance, lead with a question that they must answer in your favor to remain consistent: 'Which is more important to you, a lower price or the greater functionality?'

Quieting doubts

Emotional objections are more common from right brain personalities - the **Blues** and **Oranges.** Emotional objections are windows into the buyer's doubts about a product or service, or of your company's ability to perform, or of the suitability of the solution for the customer's needs.

For example, doubts can be around customer service. 'Can I trust you to follow through?' 'Will you really be able to provide support to all our branches?' Or they may reflect concerns about the effort needed to implement the solution: 'I'm not sure we can do this while keeping the old system going.' These are emotional objections that require you, as the sales person, to *clarify, reassure* or to *prove something*.

You must provide concrete reassurance that their concern is unfounded. For example, providing a Blue with a credible customer reference or testimonial that the Blue can identify with can go a long way towards quieting doubts. For an Orange, it's helpful to provide a third party reference that makes clear how the solution led to success or competitive advantage. Factual case studies of previous implementations can help reassure doubters that your proposal is practical and achievable.

Well done, Martha

To further illustrate redirecting, look at how my wife and I ended purchasing our dream home. When we decided we needed to move home, our real estate agent asked us the key question, 'When looking for another house, what is most important to you?' We told her that it was important that the house should be one-story, and that it had to be on the Richardson side of Springpark. That gave our agent a good start in understanding what we were looking for in our new home. Our agent found the property she thought was right for us. It met the location and was one story – but it was on the golf course and the price reflected that.

We were tempted, but responded that the house was a little big and the taxes were just a bit over our budget. So here is an example of a factual objection to this house. It's a factual concern that the size of the house and the bills that come along with it were over our planned budget.

How can a salesperson redirect or refocus based on the objection? Martha, our agent, responded by reflecting back our expressed need: 'You asked for a one story house on the Richardson side of Springpark. This property is exactly what you asked for. Yes, it might be a little bigger and more expensive than you expected because it's located on the golf course. But it's the only suitable house available in the neighborhood you requested. This is a stable neighborhood and it might be years before another like this might become available.'

Martha reminded us that the location was our principle request, our most important consideration. There was a real risk in not grabbing it. Knowing my Orange nature, she associated the decision as a contest I could win – get the house before someone else grabs it. Knowing also my wife's Orange personality, she pointed out how the layout and view of the golf course would make it a special place for entertaining our friends. Desire to stand out in entertaining is another Orange characteristic. Sold! Martha redirected us back to our principle values and the objection evaporated.

Note that Martha not only responded to our specific objections, but seized the opportunity to play to our emotional needs as Orange personalities: competitive-ness and sociability. We ended up buying the house and moving less than one mile away from the house where we had lived for fifteen years. We love our purchase to this day. Martha did not manipulate us into buying – she understood both our factual and emotional needs and used this to respond in such a way as to remove our doubts and increase the attractiveness of the opportunity. Good job, Martha.

21. CLOSING THE DEAL

Moving toward a close

As you move towards a close you need to encourage the customer to maintain progress. As you try to understand how close to a decision your customer is, and strive to address objections and clear obstacles, your company is also asking you for a realistic assessment of a closing date and probability of success. You have your hands full.

Your customer's buying decision is linked to your customer's own needs and priorities – not yours. This can sometimes lead to frustration, because the sales person does not control when the business is awarded, the customer does!

How can you move the customer forward and also provide your company with a realistic forecast? These are some of the things that will help:

Use the customer's perspective, not your own.

Understand the customer's buying process.

Engage with the customer in the earliest possible stage where they are assessing their needs and budgets.

Consider the competition.

The common theme in all of throughout: understand the personality of the customer, identify with their values, and **build a relationship**.

Try to use the **customer's perspective**, not your own, in considering the roadblocks and decision factors. Why are so many sales forecasts over-optimistic? Because the sales person tends to consider what he might do if he was in the customer's position. Instead the sales person needs to consider what the actual customer will do – and an understanding of the customer's personality style is essential to gain that perspective.

Understand the **customer's buying process**. The selling cycle you are engaged in is often just a small element in the whole buying process viewed by the customer, which may look something like this:

Identification of initial need, opportunity or challenge;

Assessment of strategic options;

Detailed needs discovery and requirements development;

Budgeting for a solution;

Engaging with multiple potential suppliers; request for information, proposal, quotation process;

Evaluating proposed solutions – both internal and external;

Making the purchasing decision;

Implementation;

Evaluation of how the solution is performing.

Your relationship with the customer, enhanced by your understanding of the personality color spectrum, will help you gather information about the customer's buying process, and at what stage the process is at any time.

Engage early in the customer's buying process. If you can become familiar with the customer's true needs up front, you can both influence the process and also benefit from a deeper understanding of the customers needs and priorities.

159

In general, if you only hear about an opportunity when the customer contacts you to get a quote, it's already too late.

Your knowledge of the opportunity should emerge from an ongoing relationship of trust, not because you received an RFP out of the blue. How often have you responded to a request for proposal you received and won? You should think about who assisted the customer in creating the RFP: possibly it was one of your competitors who helped assess the client's needs in the beginning of the customer's buying cycle.

Research the competition. Once again, your relationship with the customer will help you understand their preferences and help you form an impression of your position vis-à-vis the competition. Often you will be up against not only your usual competitors, but an internal department within the customer's organization may also be considered as a 'supplier'.

How to push. How much to push?

As salespeople, we always make the customer's deal our top priority. It's natural to think that our solution must be the customer's number one priority also! In reality the customer might view purchasing our solution – or indeed purchasing any solution – as a much lower priority. They have other things to do in their lives. The client's sense of urgency to award the business is seldom in line with our urgency for the sale. Many times sales people can not understand why the client is taking so long to make a decision on their offer when in reality the client simply has other internal considerations and other projects to address.

A sales person's desire for closure can sometimes cause stress in the sales-customer relationship, something always to be avoided.

Different personality types respond to pressure in different ways.

160

A **Blue** does not like to be pressured. Blues will take time to consult with everyone in the company who is likely to be affected by the purchasing decision. Until they are comfortable with the impact of the solution on the people in the company they will avoid making a decision. Pressing a Blue before he or she is ready will seriously damage the relationship between you and the client. To move a Blue closer to a decision, agree a period of time for consideration, and be patient. When you do attempt to close, don't ask Blues if they have decided yet; ask them if they feel ready to move forward.

To make a decision, a **Gold** needs to be very comfortable that the solution is completely right for the company: financially sound, low risk, non-disruptive and using proven technology. Golds will work to their own timetable, no matter what pressure you apply. They have a step-by-step process, so the way you move a Gold towards a close is to understand that process, and support them at every step with the information they need.

Of all the personality types, **Greens** are likely to respond least well to pressure to sign a deal. A Green will be reluctant to make a final decision until all the facts are available, and they need to have a lot more detail than others. Until you are sure you have provided all the information that a Green needs, don't ask for a close. The best approach for moving the sale forward is to ask a Green: 'What other information might you need?' and 'What will be your next step in the assessment?'

Oranges respond more positively to pressure for a close than other personality types. Oranges may well be impatient to close the deal themselves because they are always interested in quick results, always keen to move on to the next new thing. If everything is lined up to make a decision, an Orange will not prevaricate. So the way to encourage an Orange to sign is to make it easy. Discover any objections and roadblocks and clear them away. Lay out the big picture confirming that the solution makes financial sense. Point out the visible benefits that will make the Orange look good in the company. And offer a great deal.

22. CONCLUSION – NOT JUST A THEORY

The Connecting 4 People approach is highly practical:

It is straightforward to carry out an assessment.

It is possible to make a reasonable and useful initial estimation of a person's personality style during a face-to-face encounter, without running the entire test.

The color characteristics of each color makes the method easier to apply and remember.

The color guidance enables users of this method to apply the knowledge in real-life situations.

The more I use these tools the more I am convinced that this is not just another psychological theory, but a worthwhile addition to the toolkit of every one in business, and especially in sales.

We have seen how a customer starts with both *business reasons*, and *personal reasons,* to seek a new product or service. Their assessment of value is colored by both *logic and emotion*. Their selection of a product or service involves both *objective* and *subjective* factors. Sometimes it is difficult to untangle what specific thought or attitude is driving a particular behavior. To do that we would all need to become professional psychologists. But that isn't necessary if all we want to do is to serve our customers better and be successful at selling to them.

All we need to do is to become familiar with the important characteristics of each color type, assess which group our customer is in, and adjust our sales approach and communication style accordingly, throughout the sales cycle. Experienced sales people already know sales success is based on having empathy with the customer and building a strong relationship. A practical understanding of the different personality styles helps you do that.

In closing, here are some reminders about using the Connecting 4 People Assessment in your selling career.

Complete understanding of the approach takes time and effort. If you are serious about it, buy the additional materials available, learn more, and work at it.

For an accurate assessment of an individual, he or she must complete the survey form. Casual assessment in the field without the formal assessment can work really well, but should be used with care and consideration.

Use the approach to help you relate to the customer, to fine-tune your communication style, to empathize and to build relationships. Sales success will follow naturally. Don't think of this as a mechanical process.

The approach provides insights into customers' perspectives on needs, value, risk and decision-making. But this is not a rigid formula. Your customers are still people!

So now you know the **four people** and have made them your good friends! We hope you've also learned some new things about yourself as you've explored this topic. As you grow to better understand the personality styles and what they value, you can apply the methods in your everyday life to strengthen your relationships, and improve your performance in business. These friends will help you understand the perspectives, motivations and attitudes of everyone you meet in life. As a result, you will become a different salesperson, manager, team lead, and friend.

Put this to work: get out there, sell, and succeed.

About the Author

Stu Schlackman has been in sales and sales management since the early 1980s, eventually founding **Competitive Excellence**, a company that helps professionals to improve their sales and business skills through workshops that instill 'superior sales results'. His first book, *Don't Just Stand There, Sell Something*, imparts wisdom, technique and practical advice for corporate executives, sales professionals, corporate trainers and others who have the desire to compete and win in business and in life. He has also written *The 180 Rule for the Art of Connecting*.

Stu holds a degree in Mechanical Engineering from Rensselaer Polytechnic Institute and a Master of Business Administration from Kennedy Western University. He served as the 2011-2012 president for the National Speakers Association of North Texas and for the Leadership Richardson Alumni Association the same year.

He has taught business courses as the Business Division Chair for Dallas Christian College in 2008-2009. Stu also mentors students at the college. He has taught sales classes at University of Texas Dallas and has supported colleagues as a guest speaker at Southern Methodist University and Dallas Baptist University business schools. Stu is also a volunteer for the school and youth program of the Leukemia and Lymphoma Society.

Stu resides in Richardson, Texas with his wife Betty and has five children and three wonderful grandchildren. Stu remains active in his community, in business, education, and as an elder at his church.

Contact Stu and Scott at www.connecting4people.com

Made in the USA
Charleston, SC
25 January 2017